David,

Go Blue!!

WM

GO BIG or GO HOME

GO BIG or GO HOME

How the next generation of startup companies
think BIG, grow FAST, and dominate markets overnight

Wil Schroter

GO BIG
media

Go BIG Media, 1275 Kinnear Road, Columbus, OH 43212

First published in 2005 by Go BIG Media

ISBN: 1-59971-274-1

Library of Congress Cataloging-in-Publication Data

Schroter, Wil, 1974 –

    Go BIG or Go HOME : How the next generation of startup companies think BIG, grow FAST, and dominate markets overnight / Wil Schroter

Contents: Introduction – General Disclaimers – My Highlight Reel – Vision – Think BIG – Growth – Compress Time – Marketing – Act Like Number One – Capital – Create Capital – Management – Stay Small

This book is printed on radioactive paper

www.goBIGnetwork.com

This book is dedicated to those who know what it means to lie in bed at 3:00 a.m. staring at the ceiling and asking yourself:

"What the hell did I get myself into?!"

You know who you are and you'd do it again in a heartbeat.

The Table and its Contents

This book is divided into five sections. While you can choose to read it sequentially, feel free to skip around to the parts that you think you can use today. That's what I would do.

The Appetizer

15 – Introduction

A short version of why you should *"Go BIG"*, and then a much longer version. If you don't care so much about the "why" and are more concerned about the "how", jump to the first section.

25 - General Disclaimers

My shallow attempt to warn you about all of my shortcomings before reading the rest of the book. I have so many that it actually warrants its own section.

29 - My Highlight Reel

Everything you never wanted to know about my career and what I've done. If you're as cynical about business books as I am, you'll read this section and think to yourself "If he was so smart he wouldn't be wasting his time writing books." You'd be right.

The Main Course

37 - Vision – Think BIG.

There's a reason companies like Google, PayPal and Skype become huge companies in short periods of time. They think big, solve painful problems, scale quickly, address big markets and (try to) grow profitably.

79 - Growth – Compress Time.

As windows of opportunity continue to close faster, startups need to learn how to compress ten years of growth into three years by building backwards, cutting out the fat, and looking for ways to make their business scale quickly.

125 - Marketing – Act Like Number One.

Consumers have become fascinated with Number One companies, which means that if a startup expects to dominate a market, they must learn to act like a Number One company right out of the gates.

163 - Capital – Create Capital.

The cost of starting a company has plummeted, which means that startups can now create the capital they need versus spending lots of time raising it. The focus now shifts towards creating as much value as quickly as possible.

203 - Management – Stay Small.

It's all about speed versus size. Instead of trying to grow the size of the company, startups need to learn how to leverage the smallness of the company to run circles around their larger (and slower) competitors.

The Leftovers

237 - The Obligatory Epilogue

Parting thoughts as you run off into the wild blue yonder to build the next *Go BIG* company. It's really just three bits of wisdom that I often give to aspiring entrepreneurs.

239 - Shout Outs

Because the word "acknowledgements" sounds like something you offer in a eulogy. A running list of the endless number of people I have to thank.

Introduction

The short version of what I'm about to say is this:

These days successful startup companies need to think bigger, grow faster and stay smaller (physically) than ever before.

Windows of opportunity are closing faster meaning startups must react quickly to opportunities by leveraging speed versus size. In a short period of time startups need to Go BIG or go HOME!

This book is about how to Go BIG (really fast).

If that just inherently makes sense then you can probably skip the rest of what I'm about to say because you've either heard it all before or you probably just assumed everyone knew that "going BIG, fast" was the way things were done these days.

For everyone else, allow me to explain what has changed in the last few years and why companies who don't have a *Go BIG* mentality are going to get eaten alive by the ones that do.

The startup game has changed

In order to understand why it's so important to *Go BIG* you first need to understand that the game of starting companies has changed a lot in just the last few years. In particular, three important things have happened that made the startup game much easier and far more competitive at the same time.

#1: The key ingredients got cheaper

Every startup, no matter what industry they're in, has an income statement with roughly the same line items – payroll, marketing, technology and such. Ten years ago each of these line items would have cost a fortune to fund. That meant a startup company needed tons of capital in order to even make a dent in the marketplace. This created a large barrier to entry for new competitors.

However in the last few years the price of each of these key ingredients has simply plummeted, which in turn has significantly lowered the barriers to entry for startup companies.

Take a look at how each of the line items that used to break the bank for startups has changed:

Technology is a commodity. Software has gone open source (read: free), connectivity and hosting are dirt cheap and you can buy a fully functional PC on eBay for $100. Even the ridiculous costs of long distance telephone service have become a thing of the past (we love you Skype!) You can legitimately take care of all the technology startup costs for a company for about $1,000. Sweet.

Marketing became performance-based. We can thank Google and Overture for this one. With the rise of cost-per-click and search engine marketing we saw the rise of performance-based marketing that allowed companies to pay for ads that worked, not just for ads that ran. Now a startup can begin attracting customers with a marketing budget of just $100 and grow from there.

22 year olds don't make $100,000 anymore. The young, energetic talent that we all relied on to build the infrastructure behind all of our great ideas no longer has a rock star salary. The days of the HTML programmer making $100k and taking his dog to work are over. Now that work can be done for $10 per hour – or less.

Capital is less necessary. When the price of just about everything plummeted, so did the need for lots of capital. The problem with capital is that it takes time and energy to raise. Now that same time and energy can go into actually starting the company, not funding it.

When you add all of these ingredients together you get an interesting combination. All of a sudden startup companies can get to market quickly without having to raise lots of capital to do so. This breeds more startups and it breeds them a lot faster.

#2: The Internet actually happened

The promise of a billion people instantly connected to the Internet sounded like a pipe dream in the mid-90's, but guess what? It actually happened.

Today over a billion people are connected to the Internet and using it like crazy. Heck, since the Internet took off I can't even remember the last time I visited my local bank or walked into a Blockbuster to rent a movie. I don't even know if real live travel agents still exist anymore thanks to Expedia.com.

The Internet "actually happening" has meant that the benefits to having a truly networked audience can make lots of businesses highly scaleable and far more cost effective. Here are just a few of the key reasons why the proliferation of the Internet means so much:

The viral Internet got real. In the last five years we've seen the true power of viral marketing on the Internet. Companies like Napster, PayPal and MySpace have grown to tens of millions of users within just a few years simply by referral. That same rate of user acquisition a decade ago would have cost tens of millions of dollars and would have taken ten years.

A billion people actually use it. Think about this for a second. Even five years ago you had people experimenting with stuff like eBay. Today thousands of people actually make their living on eBay. When the Internet goes from a "nifty tool" to a "basic necessity" the power of that Network increases exponentially.

It scales like a mother. Once startups understood that the fastest way to grow a business is to have a truly scaleable on-line product, companies like PayPal and Google went through the roof. Sure, you can open up 20 restaurants a year, but nothing grows faster than an Internet-based company simply adding more servers to support more customers.

It's really easy to get started. Any idiot with computer and the most basic knowledge of the Web can (and has) open up shop on-line. This means that the barrier to entry for new startups has plummeted significantly (I'm still not sure if this is good or bad judging from some of the incredibly lame Web sites I've seen, but hey – who am I to judge?)

Obviously the Internet isn't new, but it's important to understand just how much it has evolved in the last five years as a key business startup tool. That is not to say that companies who do not have an Internet strategy are doomed, but it's hard to ignore an instantly addressable market of 1 billion people as a key game-changing trend.

#3: Speed became king

If the next generation of high growth startup companies has shown us anything, it's that "speed is king". Companies like Google, Skype and NetFlix have shown us that it wasn't about adding more employees and office space as quickly as possible. It was about addressing changing market conditions as quickly as possible with products that could scale big and fast.

Look at how these companies have gone from relative obscurity to market powerhouses in a matter of years, shoving giant incumbents out of their way in the process:

Google - Proved to Microsoft that being the world's largest software company was useless if you couldn't respond quickly enough to changing market conditions, like the rise in ad-supported searches. Google is now worth almost half the price of Microsoft.

Skype - Grew to over 50 million users of its voice over IP service before big telecom could even begin to respond to the opportunity (they still really haven't). Skype was sold to eBay for over $4 billion dollars after just 3 years in business.

NetFlix – Forced Blockbuster to abandon its cash cow – movie rental late fees – to try to stay competitive while NetFlix completely changed the movie rental model on them. NetFlix is now approaching 4 million subscribers and the "dark years" of late fees are now only a horror story told to young children.

What you're seeing more and more of are David and Goliath match-ups where David is kicking Goliath's proverbial ass in a pretty big way. Big companies aren't geared toward addressing rapidly changing market opportunities – startups are.

The next generation of startups has learned that it's their speed that is keeping them ahead, not their size.

The windows of opportunity are closing faster

So what does all of this mean? It means that the windows of opportunity to address new markets are closing much faster than ever before. You simply have less time to get a lot bigger than ever before.

Each of these changes will manifest itself into a handful of challenges that every startup will have to deal with.

Competition will show up faster

When you significantly reduce the barriers to entry for new companies to get to market you create more competition a lot faster. Your competition is no longer just a few well-financed companies; it's every college kid with a big idea and some time on his hands.

For you this means that your window of opportunity to be first to market is tiny at best. You don't have time to "feel the market out" and see what happens. You need to be gaining a ton of traction on Day One just to stay in the game or someone else will take your place in a heartbeat.

While the lowered cost of starting a company is great for you, it's just as great for your competition. As a result, you need to be prepared for an onslaught of competitors in a very short period of time.

Companies will grow bigger, faster

Telecom companies like Skype grew from startup to 50 million customers in less than three years. Google went from obscurity to a company with a $100 billion market cap in just a few years. The rate at which the new generation of startups can grow is astronomical.

This means that unless you are ready to grow like mad you are going to get run over by the next competitor who is. The maturity of the Internet has created a thriving platform for companies to scale quickly and cost effectively. Unless you have a plan in place to take advantage of these opportunities, you'll wind up being a footnote in the history of your industry.

Number One will take everything

Not only do startups like Google, Skype and NetFlix enjoy the spoils of new market opportunities, they also get all the attention from the people that matter most – customers, the media and investors. If you're not sure about that, can you tell me who is Number Two next to Google, Skype and NetFlix? If you're like most people you have no idea.

That's what makes these companies so successful. They get to market quickly, they claim a leadership position and they outgrow everyone else. For this reason they hog all of the attention. There's just not enough time for the world to figure out who Number Two, Three and Four even are.

So let's ask the question again – what does it all mean? It means that these days a startup has only one choice – Go BIG or Go HOME!

In order for your startup company to compete (and win, because that's what it's all about, right?) it needs to think *BIG*, grow fast, and take a Number One position before anyone can possibly challenge you.

Oh, and that all needs to be done in about three years, not ten!

The new startup playbook

Go BIG or Go HOME is a playbook for startups who want to conceive and grow companies in this new market environment.

The book is divided up into five sections that represent the key aspects of a startup company. They are in no particular order, so feel free to jump straight to any section that strikes a chord with you. The five sections look like this:

Vision – Think BIG. There's a reason companies like Google, PayPal and Skype become huge companies in short periods of time. They think big, solve painful problems, scale quickly, address big markets and (try to) grow profitably.

Growth – Compress Time. As windows of opportunity continue to close faster, startups need to learn how to compress ten years of growth into three years by building backwards, cutting out the fat, and looking for ways to make their business scale quickly.

Marketing – Act Like Number One. Consumers have become fascinated with Number One a company, which means that if a startup expects to dominate a market, they must learn to act like a Number One company right out of the gates.

Capital – Create Capital. The cost of starting a company has plummeted, which means that startups can now *create* the capital they need versus spending lots of time raising it. The focus now shifts towards creating as much value as quickly as possible.

Management – Stay Small. It's all about speed versus size. Instead of trying to grow the size of the company, startups need to learn how to leverage the smallness of the company to run circles around their larger (and slower) competitors.

Creating *Go BIG* Companies

Collectively these five sections make up the building blocks of what I call "*Go BIG* Companies". *Go BIG* companies are not about being physically big, they are about being the big players of their respective industries.

Go BIG companies are thinking bigger, growing faster and staying leaner than everyone else. Most importantly, many of the *Go BIG* companies that I reference throughout this book probably weren't around even ten years ago. They are almost all startups.

I believe that in order for the next generation of entrepreneurs to take advantage of the massive shifts that have occurred in the business marketplace we need to understand the new mechanics behind these shifts.

I hope that the lessons learned here will help you go on to create your own *"Go BIG* Company" that becomes a case study for my next book. Use what you think works and throw out the rest.

If you pick up even one point that helps your business then hopefully it was worth the read. If you end up using all of these points verbatim then I'd really appreciate a nice Christmas card in the mail (hopefully filled with some holiday stock options!) That would be good Karma, right?

Good Luck.

General Disclaimers, Apologies and Excuses

This is the part of the book where I try to warn you about all of the problems you'll probably have with me and this book as you read further. It won't make any of my writing any more valid or make you like me any more but hey - at least I was up front about my shortcomings!

I'm not an academic

I can sum up my academic experience like this – I graduated at the bottom of my High School class and got rejected from just about every college I applied to. When I finally did get into college I dropped out as soon as I had the chance and I have no plans to return anytime soon. The only time I set foot on a college campus anymore is to give lectures and to occasionally hand out scholarships (yes, I see the irony).

The advice I'm providing here stems primarily from what I've actually done or observed first hand, not from what I've researched. I've consumed as many business books as the next guy, and frankly I'm put off by authors who write about research they have done about starting companies and yet they've never actually started one.

This isn't a manifesto or an unbreakable theory. I'm not looking to "prove my colleagues wrong". It's a compilation of experiences and viewpoints that

I want to share with you in hopes that you can integrate them into your thinking and strategy.

To that end you'll find some popular items completely missing from this book – like footnotes, famous quotes and esoteric references to books you've probably never heard of. I found when writing this book that while they looked really impressive they just didn't add a lot to what I was trying to say.

If you can get over my bush league approach to academic writing you might actually dig what I'm trying to say.

I'm so not "Gestalt"

When I joined the Young Entrepreneur's Organization, which is basically group therapy for CEO's, we learned that in order to communicate with each other we would have to use a style of communication called "Gestalt Form".

The theory went that instead of saying "you should do this" when giving someone else advice you should say "what I have done in the past is this". This way you avoid telling people what to do and instead give them a scenario to understand and integrate into their own lives.

It's a really great way to get your point across and frankly I completely suck at it.

Throughout this book you'll often find me using phrases like "you should" and "you have to". I can't stand when people talk to me like this because it makes me feel like a ten year old child being scolded like a parent. Yet ironically I have a hard time getting my point across succinctly unless I break from "Gestalt Form" and simply say "You should really just do this and be done with it."

All I can say to this one is please excuse my delivery and try to see through to my intent. I want to help out if I can but by no means am I telling you what to do. Maybe ten books from now I'll be a better writer and my delivery will sync up with my intent.

This is as much as I know for now

I would love to tell you that I'm a genius who has started lots of companies and has it all figured out. I'm not and I don't.

As I've come to find out, no one else "has it all figured out" either. In fact, none of us ever "figure it all out", we just keep trying our best and hope to do a little bit better each time.

I've been starting and running companies for 12 years as of this writing. In that time I've started nine companies and worked for a few more. The only thing I know for sure is that I have far more to learn than I have to teach. This book represents what I've learned so far and I hope it helps you.

My Highlight Reel

As of the time of this writing I've done nine startups in industries ranging from software to pharmaceuticals to the arts with revenues from $10,000 per year to $600MM per year. I'm a serial entrepreneur and a startup junkie. It's hard-coded into my DNA.

What follows is a personal "highlight reel" of my career. Hopefully this will give you a sense for what I've done and where my experiences are derived from. Whether or not it establishes any credibility is anyone's guess.

Failed Miserably as a Student

I just wasn't meant to be in a classroom. I graduated at the bottom of my class in High School in Connecticut and got rejected from every college I applied to. When I finally got into college I dropped out as quickly as possible. I went to school with the intent of studying Theatre and being an actor in Hollywood. It didn't exactly pan out. Now I only act like I know what I'm talking about.

Founded Blue Diesel
(Interactive Marketing Agency)

When I was 19 I started my first company, Blue Diesel. It was the dawn of the Internet era and I was starting a Web development company. Who would have guessed? We landed huge clients - BMW, Bank One, Best Buy and Eli Lilly, grew it to $65 million in capitalized billings, and sold it to inChord communications. God bless the 90's.

Co-Founded Kelltech Internet Services
(Software, Content Management)

While still running Blue Diesel in Columbus, Ohio, I decided to co-found Kelltech Internet Services in Cleveland, Ohio. We started off doing consulting and morphed into a company with a simple content management software platform. Starting two companies in two cities wasn't exactly a picnic. Kelltech was later sold to GTCR at a value of about $10 million after three years, so we must have been on to something.

Entrepreneur of the Year Awards

I became the finalist and recipient of the Ernst & Young and U.S. Small Business Association Entrepreneur of the Year Awards in 1999 respectively. I think everyone in 1999 had +30 points added to their perceived IQ. They were all subtracted in 2001.

Joined Board of inChord Communications
(Healthcare/Pharmaceutical Ad Agency)

inChord went from being a tiny little ad agency when I joined to becoming one of the fastest growing ad agencies in the country. I had the privilege of sitting on the board while also growing one of the largest lines of business (Blue Diesel, the company I sold to them). I watched the company grow from $50 million to over $650 million in billings in five years which was a great experience.

Founded Powerhouse.com
(Real Estate Roll-up)

Great idea, no opportunity. In 1999 I co-founded Powerhouse.com to help "roll-up" 185 unsigned real estate businesses to create an $8 billion national franchise. The idea made tons of sense to the founders, just not to the 185 unsigned real estate franchises we were trying to buy. Hey, it was 1999.

Founded Atomica
(Not-for-profit Arts Organization)

Founded a not-for-profit organization to help promote the convergence of art and technology. Put on some amazing shows and events with some unbelievably talented artists. To this day I still have a hard time understanding how to ask for money with no intent on giving it back! Not-for-profit fundraising is the world's hardest job.

Ohio Businessperson of the Year Award

Named one of Ohio's most distinguished business leaders among past recipients such as Dave Thomas (Wendy's), Robert Lazarus (Lazarus Department Stores), and John McCoy (Bank One). Unfortunately you don't get a billion dollars to go with it like they did.

Joined Swapalease as CEO
(Automotive Leasing Marketplace)

Joined Swapalease.com as the CEO and learned how the auto industry works. Within a few years we became the world's largest auto leasing marketplace with over $1 billion in vehicles listed. I also learned how to negotiate a better lease only to confirm my suspicions that you really *do* get screwed when buying a car.

Opened a Nightclub
(Entertainment Industry)

Had a stupid idea while nursing a post-New Year's hang over that it would be nice to have a party like New Year's *every* weekend. Six weeks later we opened up "Status", a nightclub that held about a thousand people and was home to acts such as Danny Howells and the Crystal Method. Closed it the same year. Somehow working from 8 a.m. on Friday (at my regular job) and then on til 4 a.m. Saturday got old really quick.

Launched LeasePower
(Financial Services)

While growing Swapalease we realized there was a great opportunity to lease new cars, not just transfer existing leases. So we launched LeasePower. You could pick a car, choose a lease payment, and apply for financing right on-line. It turned out to be a great service for people to get a price low enough to take to a dealer instead of using us. We rolled it back into Swapalease.

Won the WWF Intercontinental Championship

Okay, this never really happened. I just wanted to see if anyone was even paying attention at this point. Plus, it was kind of fun to pretend for a moment that it actually happened. I always wanted to be the next Tito Santana – "Ariba!"

Published *LeaseAdvisor*

Wrote an entire book about how to lease a car. Sold pretty well, primarily through Swapalease.com. If you ever find yourself suffering from insomnia, I highly recommend reading (or writing) a book about leasing a car.

Launched the Go BIG Network
(Business to Business E-commerce)

Created an on-line marketplace to connect startup companies, investors, advisors and service providers in real time. I actually got the idea for the company while writing this book. Since then I've had the opportunity to see thousands of business ideas from early concepts to actual implementations. It's like being at the Grand Central Station of entrepreneurship.

Became a nationally syndicated columnist
(Media Industry)

In preparation for writing a book I asked American City Business Journals if they would let me author a bi-weekly column about starting companies and raising money. Within the first year the column would go on to get syndicated in 42 markets reaching out to over 4 million business owners which was really cool.

Wrote a book about starting startups called *Go BIG or Go HOME!*
(Publishing Industry)

The publishing industry is one of the most antiquated, backwards industries I've come across. I say this having been rejected by just about every big publishing house out there for this book, so you can appreciate my bent. In case you're thinking about writing a book, my only advice is to find a publisher that will let you keep more than $1 per book in royalties. First time authors get screwed. There, I said it.

Vision.

Think BIG

Have you every wondered why some startup companies attract loads of investment capital, lure the best people, and land huge customers while others seem to wallow in obscurity?

If you think about it all startup companies begin with the same things – an entrepreneur, an idea, and maybe a business plan. Yet something happens between the time when they conceive this idea and the time in which the idea becomes a great company that causes some companies to *Go BIG*, and other companies to go home.

The difference between those companies is their ability to "think big". You don't create billion-dollar behemoths like Google, PayPal, and NetFlix in a matter of years (as opposed to decades) without thinking in much bigger terms than everyone else.

What these companies (and many others just like them) have done is come to the table with a vision that demands big thinking. These companies create and dominate markets overnight. They change the way people consume products and behave. They attract the biggest investors, land the biggest customers, and, in the end, get rewarded with massive payouts.

To the casual observer these companies might all seem like a fluke, perhaps a throwback to the Internet era or a lottery ticket that some entrepreneur just happened to pull at the right time.

And maybe you could consider them a fluke if it weren't for the fact that it's happening over and over, and it's happening more often as time goes by. This next generation of startup companies – Google, PayPal, and NetFlix (among others) – represent a generation of startups that grow like crazy because they are conceived and architected to grow bigger and faster than ever.

This section is about the very foundation of these companies – the vision. It's about how entrepreneurs are approaching markets with much larger expectations. It's about how the market itself – the investors, customers, even the media – have come to expect bigger ideas and bigger companies to be created in record time.

While big visions may come from a variety of different companies and industries they all seem to share a few traits among them. They tend to solve painful problems, scale quickly, address big markets, and hope to hell they do it all profitably.

In this section we're going to take a look at how companies build their vision from the ground up by taking these factors into consideration from inception. Then we're going to figure out how to apply them to our own business models.

Chapter 1

Solve Painful Problems

Above all else high-growth companies must solve painful problems. These are problems so pressing that a customer is compelled to spend money on your product to solve them. And the greater the pain the customer feels, the more they're willing to pay.

You would think *Go BIG* companies focus all of their time and attention on coming up with the best *solutions* in the market. That's not the case. These companies start with understanding the *problem* better than anyone else. They leverage this understanding to create a position in the marketplace that focuses entirely on the severity of the problem.

The success of just about any *Go BIG* company can easily be mapped back to their ability to solve painful problems. Whether it's Match.com solving the problem of being lonely or eBay solving the problem of imperfect marketplaces, there's always an underlying issue that causes customers to flock to their respective services.

Swapalease: An exchange of problems

At Swapalease.com, we knew that the average person stuck in a car lease would have to shell out $6,000 to terminate their car lease early. Standard lease contracts state that if you want to walk away from your lease you are required to make every last payment, regardless of how far into your lease you are.

Let me give you an example of how painful that problem can be. Imagine that you just lost your job and that shiny new BMW you thought would be the pimp ride is now a $500 per month liability in your driveway. You're six months into a three year lease and sitting on a massive $15,000 liability.

Along comes Swapalease.com, a marketplace for auto lease transfers. The company connects people who want to get out of a car lease with people who want to get into a car lease. You can list your car on the site for less than $100 and transfer your vehicle to someone else who assumes all obligations of your lease. You walk away lease-free for about one hundred bucks - much less painful than fifteen grand.

www.swapalease.com

What makes Swapalease.com valuable as a business isn't a fancy website or sweet marketing. It's the fact that it solves an enormous problem that people have. More importantly, it solves a problem that people are willing to pay money to fix.

Translating the pain of the problem into the solution involves two steps. The first step is to define the problem well by understanding the size of the problem, the severity of the problem, and the likely alternatives.

Once you've determined the problem is real, the second step is to translate the size of the problem into the monetary value of the solution.

Start with the severity

The severity of the problem your company solves should be the very essence of the value your solution provides. That's a somewhat fancy way of saying "if people have a big problem and you have a great solution, you're on the right track!"

At Swapalease.com we can point to the severity of the problem numerically – an average cost of about $6,000 to walk away from your lease if you simply try to pay off the difference you owe. Beyond that it's not as though the customer gets something tangible for their six grand – they simply get the luxury of *not* paying for the rest of their lease.

The severity of this problem completely drives the value of the Swapalease.com solution. If the average consumer could simply sell their car outright and walk away without much of a penalty (like you can with a car loan) the problem would not be nearly as severe, meaning our solution wouldn't be as valuable.

Perhaps the severity of the problem your customers have is not so quantifiable in numeric terms, like price. That's fine as long as you can create an accurate description of how that problem truly affects the customer and why they need a solution so badly.

Even severity is a relative term. For some of the customers at Swapalease the cost of $6,000 is all the money in the world, while others think it's a small price to pay to make a lifestyle change for their vehicle (I personally think it's a lot of money no matter how you slice it!). The challenge is to align the severity of the problem with the customers who share your pain.

Match.com: The Perfect Relationship

Maybe your product provides a solution to an emotional problem like relationships. A company like Match.com, the popular Internet dating site, doesn't provide the solution to a financial problem (unless you find and marry some rich person on the site). They provide the solution to an emotional problem. But they understand the severity of that problem pretty well.

Being in the "dating scene" is uncomfortable for most people especially as they get older and spend far less time in nightclubs, bars, or the single social scene as a whole. Nothing sucks more than coming home on a Friday night and having no messages on your answering machine. Being lonely is a strong emotional problem with which people can readily identify.

Match.com realizes that if someone is distressed about being unable to find the right relationship in their life, that it's probably worth something to them (about $20 per month, according to their site) to help fix that problem. They can connect the emotional needs of their customers to an agreeable price point.

www.match.com

That's what finding the severity of the problem is all about – matching the market need with the value. Your ability to dive in and understand exactly how big the problem is and how it affects your customer at all levels (emotionally, financially, etc.) will help you develop a product solution that rings true with your customers.

Recommendations:

- Understand the problem. Write down in explicit detail the exact problem your customer has and how it makes them feel. The more detail you can provide about the problem the more valuable your solution will appear.

- Compare the severity of the problem to the value of the solution. Ideally you would like your solution to be a very simple answer to an enormous problem. The greater the distance between the size of their problem and the value of your solution the more attractive your product will be. Think of Swapalease.com – we get rid of $6,000 of debt for $100.

Size up the problem

Illustrating the severity of the problem only illuminates part of the picture – the fact that a potential customer would be interested in our solution. You still need to demonstrate that the problem is bigger than just one person.

Sizing up the market for the problem gives you a much better indication of whether your business idea has merit. For instance, we know there are more than 16 million active car leases on the road at any given time. Research shows that 1 in 3 people are interested in getting out of their lease. This leaves a market size of over 5 million people who are stuck in a $6,000 commitment and want to get out. That's a lot of big problems for a heck of a lot people.

Ideally you're looking for a severe problem that affects a huge audience. If instead of tackling the auto leasing industry we tackled the heavy equipment leasing industry, we may have solved a huge problem, but the market for that problem would have been significantly smaller, simultaneously making our opportunity a lot smaller.

Finding the right market for your product is a delicate balancing act between finding a market that is well-targeted and an audience that is big. We could easily expand the size of the Swapalease.com market to include everyone that is even *buying* a car. Theoretically anyone willing to take out a car loan may be willing to assume a lease. So we could expand our market to include the 40 million people in the market to buy a car at any time.

The problem with that line of thinking is that it doesn't represent the audience who truly has the problem. The problem lies among the 5 million people who are already leasing a car, *and* want to get out of the car at some point. Everyone else has plenty of alternatives, meaning Swapalease.com is less valuable to them.

There's no specific math here, but the general goal is to find an audience that is as big as possible yet still has a demonstrable market *need* for your product.

Recommendations:

- Look for the larger application of the problem. If it's severe and affects a huge audience, you're on the right track. If it looks like the problem only affects a select group of people, you may not have much opportunity to grow the business in the future.

- Try to focus the "size of the audience" to the folks who actually need your product instead of every person who could ever possibly consume your product. The further you reach out to a larger audience the less impact your product is likely to have on those customers. It's better to have a big impact on a small audience than very little impact on a huge audience.

Compare the solution to the alternatives

In most cases, once you've determined the severity and size of a problem, the solution presents itself. In the case of Swapalease.com, the obvious solution was: offer people a significantly cheaper way out of their auto leases. But shaping this solution requires some sanity checking.

The next step is to compare your solution to the alternatives. All things being equal, if your solution is more accessible, cheaper, better, or (in the case of Microsoft) more effectively marketed, people will buy from you. You need to understand the customers' alternatives to buying your product in order to understand how valuable your product really is.

At Swapalease.com it costs less than $100 to list your car and walk away from your lease by transferring the obligation to someone else. Compare that to the $6,000 you will have to pay to the leasing company or the $500 you will pay next month as your lease payment and the solution seems rather attractive.

If the price of Swapalease.com were $5,000, the contrast in value wouldn't be quite as great, although one could argue it's still cheaper. *Go BIG* companies look for solutions that not only solve problems, but create real obvious (and much better!) alternatives.

Don't assume price is the only driving factor, though. Other factors like how accessible you are, how well customers associate with your brand, or even how friendly your staff is can make your product a more suitable alternative.

Swapalease.com has competitors that actually give away the same product for free. From a pricing standpoint Swapalease isn't the cheapest in town, but it is the most effective solution. These customers have plenty of alternatives that are cheaper and just as accessible but less valuable because of the fact that Swapalease actually transfer more leases than they do.

Compare your solution to all of the available alternatives: price, brand, location, or whatever your customer's decisions are based upon. You need to understand which set of circumstances presents your solution as the best alternative. *That's* the target market you want to zero in on right away.

Recommendation:

- List all of the possible alternatives you customer currently has to solving their problem. Rate the value of your solution (compared to the alternatives) on a scale of 1 to 5. Then look at your list and figure out where you score the best. That's where you want to begin solving your problem.

Summary

Go BIG companies are constantly on the hunt for the "perfect problem" – one that is incredibly painful for lots of people and has few (if any) alternatives. Here are a few quick examples of *Go BIG* companies who were able to hit all three metrics right nose:

Google – The Search Giant

- *Big problem:* Finding what you are looking for on the Internet is incredibly difficult (too much information, arrrrrgh!).

- *Big market:* A billion people using the Internet with 85% of Web pages found with the help of a search.

- *Alternatives:* Existing search engines "found" websites but did a lousy job of ranking them so that the "good stuff" rose to the top. Google launched a simple search engine that provided the best results on a consistent basis.

PayPal – Money for Nothing

- *Big problem:* It's hard to buy something from someone else (like you do on eBay) if you can't take a credit card or easily wire money.

- *Big market:* eBay has over 150 million people buying and selling stuff online.

- *Alternatives:* Before PayPal people needed to use wire services which were complicated and expensive. PayPal made it easy for people to simply "email" money to other people via the Web.

LowerMyBills.com – Being cheap for a living

- *Big problem*: Most bills people pay are commodity services – phone service, credit cards, insurance, etc. There are almost always comparable solutions at a cheaper rate that people would love to know about.

- *Big market*: Just about every person on the planet, but particularly people who are watching their money closely.

- *Alternatives*: You could call around and do all of your homework and shop the lowest rate for everything yourself, but it's free to do it all at once on LowermyBills.com, so why bother?

Chapter 2

Scale Quickly

In this book I spend a lot of time talking about scaling versus growing the business. That's because *Go BIG* companies don't just grow at a measured pace, they scale exponentially to billion-dollar behemoths in virtually no time. *Go BIG* companies not only look for big problems to solve, they develop business models that can simultaneously support this overnight growth.

First let me explain how growing and scaling are different. Growing implies that you are adding more resources (people, facilities, etc.) at about the same rate you are adding more revenue. Professional services companies are notorious for expanding this way because they tend to add more people for every extra dollar that they earn. That's not a very scaleable model.

I've spent almost a decade running professional services companies both large and small, and I can tell you first hand that they are fun to grow, but hard to scale. I spent countless hours trying to figure out why these types of companies could grow quickly but couldn't seem to scale like software companies or Internet-based companies. Here's my experience with this problem:

inChord: Not Ready for Scale

While on the board of inChord, a large healthcare advertising agency, I watched our fledgling agency go from a few dozen employees and a few million dollars in revenue to over 500 employees and $100 million in revenue in about four years.

By most people's accounts, our growth was admirable. But the problem was that the business wasn't scalable. No matter how hard we tried, nothing could change the fact that bringing in more revenue always meant hiring more people.

And hiring more people took lots of time and much of that money we were bringing in. In one year we hired a person every single work day of the year, and it still wasn't fast enough to satisfy the demand for our services.

In addition to not scaling the people fast enough, we couldn't leverage the product. Each advertising campaign had to be developed from the ground up. So going from $25 million in sales was just as resource intensive (people, time, etc.) and costly as going to $50 million in sales. We generated more revenue, and more profit, but the two were always directly proportional to each other.

www.inchord.com

And that was the problem – we had growth, but we didn't have scale. Our model was designed to grow at a healthy pace year after year, adding sales and adding infrastructure as we went along, but not to scale.

Scale is where it's at

Scale provides the ability to grow revenues much faster and more efficiently than you grow your infrastructure. In the above example imagine if we were selling a software product and not an hour of someone's time while experiencing the same type of growth. As more opportunities to sell the product presented themselves, we wouldn't incur the development costs each time. Therefore as revenue grew steadily, profits would grow exponentially.

Companies like Google, eBay, and PayPal rely on scalability to become billion-dollar players in short periods of time. These companies have figured out that being able to deliver the product to one person or one hundred people in roughly the same time at roughly the same cost would allow them to attack big markets quickly and cheaply.

At inChord, if we could have built the product once and then delivered it to additional clients at a minimal cost of time and resources, we would have been a billion-dollar company. Instead, we were forced to curb our growth because we didn't have a business model that would allow us to scale faster.

What we needed was a business model that would have allowed us to add $100 million in revenue as fast as we could have added $10 million. The reason *Go BIG* companies get around this problem is because they are designed from the ground up to scale their infrastructure as fast as their revenues.

MySpace: Designed to Scale

Social networking services like MySpace enable users of the site to connect with friends and colleagues, forming circles of relationships online. Users hop on the site, create profiles and invite their friends to join the site and create their own profiles. Over time your friends will invite other friends to join and you can create a vast network of people who know each other and can share common interests. It's known as a "social network."

People use social networking sites to do anything from finding dates to finding potential business partners. A company like MySpace is geared toward social relationships of people with common interests, such as people interested in the music group Green Day.

All the while MySpace is investing very little cash to benefit from this growth. Additional marketing money is rarely needed because the users fuel the marketing by inviting their friends. At the same time the incremental cost to service an additional user is limited to small amount of additional hard disk space.

www.myspace.com

MySpace grew so quickly that within three years of operation the company was sold to News Corporation for over $570 million. To give you a sense for how quickly the company grew, according to ComScore the site drew over 17.7 million visitors in June/2005, up from just 1.2 million in June/2004 – that's a 1,400% growth rate!

There's a reason MySpace was able to grow so fast (and become so valuable) so quickly. The company was built from the ground up with scalability in mind.

Let's dig a little deeper to see how they did it.

Scale Point #1: Cost of Incremental Sale

MySpace has a scalable cost of incremental sale. So do companies like eBay, Google, and PayPal, all of whom rely primarily on adding servers or some other relatively cheap infrastructure item to serve a growing user base.

Contrast that to our growth model at inChord. Every time we added another dollar in revenue we had to pay almost a dollar in resource cost. The same problem exists whether we're at $1 million in revenue or $100 million.

If your cost of sales is not decreasing as you add more customers, it's likely that you have a business model that just isn't scalable. You need to find a way to deliver the product to your next customer at a lower cost than previous customers.

Recommendation:

- Look for some aspect of your business that can be created once and sold many times. It could be a piece of intellectual property (like a market report), a method (like the formula for how you solved a client's problem), or the solution itself (you can re-sell the e-commerce software you built for a client).

Scale Point #2: Speed of Growth

The speed of growth at MySpace is lightning quick because it takes very little time to add an additional customer and marginal resources to service an additional customer.

If MySpace had to add another customer support person for every ten people that signed up for the service, their cost of operations would skyrocket and their rate of growth would be severely limited by the time it would take to add those additional people.

When contemplating your business model, the speed at which you can grow is an important aspect of the plan. If you cannot grow the infrastructure of the company to keep up with demand, your customers will inevitably find another company that can.

While you may not have a very efficient production or delivery method now, you must account for how you plan on improving these processes in the not-too-distant future. Some models are inherently fast – like adding more classified ads to an online site. Other models require some substantial expertise in production and logistics, like selling millions of books online (think Amazon).

Go BIG companies move so quickly because they have forecasted how they will be able to keep up with exponential demand for the future. It's hard to become a giant like Amazon without devising a pretty slick growth model behind the scenes.

Recommendation:

- Drill down into the timeline of your product or service delivery. Consider what it will take to deliver your product (cost, time, etc.) on both a small scale and a very large scale. You need to think through the entire process of a 3-5 year plan to understand how quickly you can really grow.

Scale Point #3: Cost per Acquisition

Your cost per acquisition (CPA) is your total cost of sales and marketing to acquire a customer. If your CPA increases dramatically as your model grows, you're in for some tough times ahead.

For example, if you can acquire your first customer for $5 and you earn $15 on the sale (a $10 profit), it's all good. This is often the case with your first few customers, as they are often people you know or customers that are easy to reach – the "low hanging fruit", if you will.

Once you run out of these customers though, you start to get into the customers that are harder to reach and because of that, require more cash to reach. Now if you find it costs you $20 in marketing dollars to earn $15 in revenue, you've got a big problem on your hands.

However, if you're a company like MySpace, your CPA actually *decreases* over time, as your additional customers are acquired via invites from your existing subscribers. This provides for a lot of scalability because you are not constrained by available marketing capital.

CPA is probably the most contentious metric in any model. Few companies are able to quantify their CPA, let alone lower it. Your goal in creating a business that can scale is finding a way to keep your CPA down over time, thus keeping your profitability up.

Recommendation:

• Figure out how big you can get with a relatively low CPA. When the CPA starts to rise, are there are any other opportunities available to you to create a higher margin to account for the increase? For example, can you charge more for your product as your company gets bigger? Managing your CPA as your company grows is critical, so keep it top of mind.

Scale Point #4: Market Leverage

Market leverage is both a scaling point and an incredibly powerful competitive advantage. Market leverage means that as you get bigger, the value of your service increases while decreasing the value of a competing service.

eBay is a great example of market leverage in action. What motivates sellers to sell stuff on eBay (and not another auction site) is they can address the largest audience of buyers at one time. This significantly *increases* the chances of selling their item.

At the same time, each item that gets added to the site attracts more buyers with the incentive of a large, consolidated inventory. Over time, the market itself becomes the leverage point. The biggest market creates the most value to buyers and sellers.

Economists identified a similar phenomenon when the telephone was introduced. As more people had telephones, you had the potential to contact more people, which created more incentive to join the network.

MySpace shares this same characteristic. The more users that join, the more valuable the community is to additional users that join. Creating market leverage in your own business model will allow you to ward off competitors and drive up the value of your product at the same time.

Recommendations:

- Identify the aspects of your business that increase in value to your customer as more customers are added or the service gets larger. What can a customer contribute by using your service that will add more value to the next customer behind them? That's where you find your market leverage.

Summary

Ideally you're creating a business model that can scale on all four of the previous points just like MySpace can. It's not necessary to hit all four, but doing so increases your chances for success.

We're going to spend a lot more time discussing the speed and rate of growth in the section appropriately entitled "Growth", but for now just keep in mind that a company that is designed to *Go BIG* is literally *designed* from the ground up to scale quickly.

Chapter 3

Address Big Markets

Another reason companies can *Go BIG* is because they address big markets. It's impossible to become a billion-dollar company if your vision is for a product that can only service a $10 million market.

Though it's important for your business to have access to large markets, that doesn't mean you should attack the entire market at once. Amazon started by selling books before it branched into other retail categories. Yahoo! started by providing a directory of links before it became a blue-chip media company. And eBay was a haven for collectors trading PEZ dispensers before it became the world's online auction marketplace.

The point is that each company had a vision to address a very large market, but they started by servicing a smaller segment of the market very well. Their solutions worked well on a small scale to get them started and they had enough room to expand to a billion-dollar scale.

The Importance of Running Room

Running room is a term venture capitalists use to refer to a company's market potential. If your vision is to service a market that could one day be worth over $1 million that's not going to provide a great deal of running room. Even if you're able to corner 99% of the market quickly, the market won't necessarily continue to grow.

In many cases it's possible for investors to look down the road and determine that there is a limit to the potential size of the market. That's the death toll for startups because their entire valuation is based upon their ability to become exponentially bigger in the near future, not constrained by customer availability or interest.

It's a slippery slope, though. While you want to have a great deal of opportunity for expansion, you don't want to address a market that's so big that you couldn't possibly wrap your arms around it. Most often companies err on the side of addressing markets that are too small, especially in the formative stages when "taking on the world" seems like too big of a task.

You need to strike the fine balance between finding a market that is big enough to give you plenty of room to run in the not-too-distant future and a market that's worth pursuing at all.

Perhaps the best way to explain the importance of running room in a startup company is to demonstrate what happens when you run out of it. A great example of a business that ran out of running room is that of Autobytel, the popular online car shopping service.

Autobytel: Out of Gas

Autobytel started out as a great idea. Car-buying customers were going to the Internet to research their car purchases and to avoid getting "taken" by a car dealer. Autobytel stepped in to help them find the necessary information they needed.

By virtue of being an important information resource, Autobytel could become a middleman between the car-buying consumer and the dealer. If a consumer was looking for information on a car, Autobytel would provide that information and then suggest a dealer in their area that could provide the vehicle.

On the back end Autobytel would approach car dealers and sell them these customer leads. Compared to uncertain ways of generating customers such as billboards and newspapers, this seemed like an efficient and reliable alternative for dealers to find new customers.

From the onset it looked like the business could grow forever. There are 20,000 car dealers in North America with an insatiable appetite for new business (and presumably buying car leads) and the consumer demand for pre-purchase research was going through the roof. Autobytel went public soon after and the stock soared.

But as often happens with a successful service, Autobytel attracted competitors. Soon Autobytel was competing for the same dealers and the same consumers. Their share of the market was being quickly eroded by competitors such as Cars.com, Auto Trader, and Edmunds.com. *(continued)*

At the same time the market itself was losing steam. It turned out that few dealers were having success with the "Internet Leads" because those customers were too educated about buying cars which meant lower margins on the sale of cars.

Consumer sentiment also changed. Consumers began to feel that these auto research sites were just thinly-veiled attempts to drive them to a dealer and became more skeptical about submitting their contact information.

The growth potential for Autobytel's model began evaporating right in front of their eyes. Investors took notice quickly and Autobytel's share price plummeted into the single digits. It's hard to invest in a company that has no way of proving that it can grow.

www.autobytel.com

Autobytel is an example of a great concept that is very scalable, highly profitable, and well-targeted but lacks running room. In any stage of a company's life, once the potential to grow is gone the value drops like a rock.

Some of this thinking might sound counter-intuitive. You may be thinking "isn't owning 100% of my market my goal?" and the answer would be "no". At which point you control 100% of your market you no longer have plenty of room for expansion. Not to mention, the Department of Justice seems to have some sort of problem with the whole concept of monopolies!

If it looks like you're in a position to own 100% of your market, the most logical step would be to expand your market to include a broader customer base.

Thinking Big and Starting Small

So does this mean you should look for the biggest possible market and tell the world you're going to tackle it? No.

Addressing big markets is a balancing act between finding a market you can wrap your arms around effectively in the short term while still providing enough room in the future so that you can grow indefinitely. This strategy for addressing your market requires a two-stage approach – a short-term strategy and one for expansion.

The short game

The short-term strategy is your plan to get to market in the next eighteen to thirty-six months. This involves targeting a smaller, focused group of customers and creating a name for yourself.

In the case of Autobytel their short game was right on track. They were able to quickly take a leadership position in automotive lead generation. If they lost focus in the short term by also trying to be a proxy to consumers buying homes, insurance, or mortgages they would have likely had difficulty concentrating their resources effectively. This would have compromised their early success.

Lots of startups try to be too much too quickly and it often keeps them from becoming anything at all. Your resources are limited early on, so you need to make the best use of them. This means focusing on a narrowly-targeted market. Frankly, if you can't get past the short game, it doesn't matter if you have an expanded strategy – you won't be around long enough to use it.

Recommendations:

- Keep your short-term strategy focused on dominating a concentrated market area. Your goal is to create momentum for your company and build infrastructure that will parlay well into a larger market.

- Make sure your plan covers getting *past* your short game. If it takes you 10 years to get past your short-term strategies it's likely the bigger opportunity will be long gone.

The expanded strategy

The expanded strategy details your plan to bring your company into a bigger market. It also assumes that you have succeeded at making a name for yourself in the short-term stage.

Your expanded strategy takes advantage of the momentum you created in your short game. Amazon used its success in the books market to expand quickly into videos and music which were an obvious fit. This also broadened the market opportunity for the company, providing additional running room.

The expanded strategy also presumes that there is some sort of bridge between what you were successful at in the short term and what you will also be good at in the long term.

In the case of Autobytel, once they had some traction in the short game they would have been better served to expand into similar markets quickly. They may have created an online auction service (like eBay motors) or perhaps developed software programs to help dealers market more effectively. (They did, but they didn't do enough of it.)

Just as trying to bite off too much too early can keep you from getting started, staying too small when it's time to grow (as Autobytel did) can also inhibit your long-term opportunities.

Recommendation:

- Your expanded strategy is only as good as the scope of opportunity your short-term strategy has created for you. If you want to be the world's largest auction marketplace, your short-term strategy would be to tackle a market (like PEZ dispensers or trading cards) that allows you to create the software you need to run this marketplace. Your expanded strategy would then leverage this software to tackle additional markets (like eBay has) quickly.

Summary

Addressing big markets is all about going after the biggest pie but starting off only taking small bites you can swallow. Look for big markets that can be addressed incrementally. Put yourself in the position to address those markets by tackling smaller problems extremely well and using that momentum to become a bigger player.

Most companies do very well at attacking small markets but never parlay that success into creating bigger opportunities. Wal-Mart would have stayed a small rural department store if Sam Walton hadn't converted its success into a national chain.

You don't need to get crazy with the idea of attacking a big market. Again, your goal is to create enough of an opportunity to grow but simply start with an opportunity that you can tackle effectively.

Chapter 4

Grow Profitably

As obvious as "being profitable" might seem as a success benchmark, it's amazing how many companies overlook it. The age-old "we'll get big now and figure out how to be profitable later" approach may have worked well in the 1990s when you could go public before anyone figured out your business didn't work, but it doesn't fly anymore. The world is much wiser, or so I'm told.

All the other aspects of growing like crazy are useless if you can't turn all that growth into a profit. If you're not sure how important profit is, hop over to FuckedCompany.com and scan the tombstones of hundreds of companies who thought they could find away around this little nuisance called "profitability."

You may stop for a moment and say to yourself "Wil's full of it. Lots of high growth companies succeed by growing now and making money later, just look at every startup in Silicon Valley (the Valley seems to have a strange love for unprofitable companies)." You would be right, many companies do grow on an early "no-profit" strategy, but more often than not this strategy is a thinly veiled excuse for a company not being able to execute on their business model properly. So I'm going to be the advocate of profitability here. Let's see if I can make a case for you.

Profitability = Sustainability

You may be able to achieve growth in the short term and even tolerate losses, but if your business doesn't have a sustainable way to turn a profit, you're screwed.

I can sell dollar bills for 99 cents and grow like crazy, address a huge market, and solve a painful problem, but rest assured I'll go out of business in the process!

Startup companies often sustain losses at the expense of growth in the short term. Many businesses don't show profit growth until they scale to a significant size. But if they don't (or more importantly, can't) get to that size quickly, their operational expenses will eventually put them out of business.

Creating a sustainable enterprise is the basis not only for validating your business model, but allowing you to make smart, strategic choices versus really bad, desperate choices. There's nothing more confident than a company that can stand on its own without anyone's help.

Getting to the point of profitability, or at the very least sustainability (which I would define as a point in time where you don't have to raise any more capital) is a critical step in the formative stages of a startup company. I know I sound like an old, curmudgeon CFO when I say this, but nothing validates the success of a company and the capability of its managers like a healthy balance sheet.

In order to make my point, let me give you a sense for what happens to a company that has great ideas and plenty of funding but just simply loses sight of staying sustainable (I'm not even saying profitable!) long enough to become a real company.

Kozmo: We offer everything but a profit

Kozmo was a great idea and a very cool service. The company was created in 1998 by Joseph Park and Yong Kang to deliver small goods free of charge, all purchased online. Think your corner grocery store with free delivery.

The company raised a staggering $280 million and was out of business just three years after they launched. I'm no CFO and somehow I don't understand how you could go out of business with $280 million in cash lying around, but Kozmo pulled it off brilliantly.

Back to the point. Kozmo had everything you could want in a *Go BIG* company. In fact, let's review the checklist to make sure:

- Solves a painful problem? Check. Many people prefer the ease of online shopping, but they also desire the instant gratification of retail shopping.
- Addresses a big market? Check. Everyone needs ice cream.
- Scales like crazy? Check. One website will work in every city.
- Grows profitably? Not so much.

Customers loved Kozmo, but the margins were so thin that the company couldn't operate profitably. There's a reason you have to go Wal-Mart to buy ice cream – because Sam Walton couldn't figure out a way to drive it to your house for the same price!

Great ideas aren't great companies unless that great idea generates a profit. Kozmo was one of the best examples in recent history of a company that was genuinely meeting an important market need, just not one that could be addressed profitably.

Growth Should Beget Profitability

The purpose of scaling a business is to become more profitable. If your business doesn't generate a profit on a small scale, it isn't likely that increasing the size of the company will do anything but increase the size of the problem.

Some models need a little scale to be worth anything. Manufacturers or other operations with large capital costs need to sell large volumes of product to recover their initial costs at a price that's reasonable to the customer.

Other business models require a certain amount of volume or customers to have any value. It'd be hard to make a dollar at eBay if there were only a handful of visitors. It needs to scale a bit for the marketplace to have value.

When there's an obvious correlation between necessary scale and profit, you're in good shape. But there should be a clear pattern that demonstrates that as you get bigger, your profitability is as certain as possible. It's flat-out irresponsible to grow a company just for the sake of growth in hopes that one day profitability will find its way to your door.

Recommendation:

- Analyze your growth projections. Does scaling really make you more profitable or just bigger? Make sure you understand when profit requires scale and when the two are independent.

Don't Confuse Popular with Profitable

Just because everyone loves your product and you're gaining customers, it doesn't mean profitability is inevitable. This is especially true if you're not charging anything. In that case attracting droves of excited customers makes it easy to forget that those "customers" aren't making you any money.

Napster: Very cool, very broke

The Napster story is a great example of a company that was wildly popular, heavily trafficked, and completely profit-free. The company, launched in 1999, allowed users to share files (primarily music MP3s) among each other in a simple-to-use system.

In just over two years the number of worldwide users peaked at 26.4 million. Napster was everywhere and was considered one of the most popular and fastest-growing software products in history.

The problem was they never had any way to make money. What drove customers to the Napster product was the opportunity to get free music quickly and easily, not to pay fees in the process.

Napster's eventual demise was due to a massive lawsuit by artists and the RIAA. Despite the lawsuit, the company never had a revenue model that could convert its popularity into riches.

www.napster.com

Providing a product or service for free is the job of a not-for-profit organization – not an incorporated company. If you expect to create value in the long term, you need to be able to turn your growth in *popularity* into a plan to grow *profitability*.

If your product offering has value, charge for it. Swapalease.com could easily give away our car listings for free and be ten times the size they are, but they don't because they know that if they are providing value they need to be earning revenue. It's a pretty simple equation, really.

Recommendations:

- Look for the aspects of your offering that generate consumer popularity, and that customers are willing to pay for. If you can't envision a way to make money, re-classify the company as a 501(c)3 "not-for-profit" organization because effectively you're a charity, not a business. At least you'll get a tax break.

Giving it away for free isn't a Business Model

If you give your product or service away to would-be customers, you set a dangerous precedent that you're willing to give it away forever. As I've said before: if a customer isn't paying for your product in some way, shape, or form, you're not running a business.

Getting a customer to use your product for free only proves a customer's willingness to pay nothing. True value is established when a customer forks over a dollar (or lots of them) for your product.

Netscape: The Founders of Free

In 1994 Netscape Communications went to market with one of the most powerful applications ever released – the Web browser. Dubbed "Netscape Navigator" the software became one of the most widely- and rapidly-adopted applications ever released. It was truly a cool product that turned most of the world onto the World Wide Web.

What really drove the adoption of the browser was the fact that it was free. Prior to distributing applications via the Internet, companies had to use traditional retail channels to get their applications to market. This was costly and time-intensive, so giving them away was rarely the distribution mechanism of choice.

Netscape, however, decided to do just that – they allowed users to download their browser for free. Since they didn't share the distribution costs of traditional retail and physical channels, this was a cost-effective way to grow market share.

In the process Netscape did two things really well – they increased the adoption of their product, and they set the price the customer was willing to pay for a Web browser application to zero. After that the market for selling Web browser software disappeared almost completely.

www.netscape.com

How could Netscape invent one of the most popular and widely adopted software applications in history and at the same time never make any real money at it? Simple – they established the price at "zero."

Getting customers to go from "free" to "paid" is extremely difficult to do. Companies establish the value of their product mostly from the price they set for their product. Does a Bentley Continental GT really cost $160,000 to build? No, but if Bentley sold the Continental for $20,000 there's no way they would be able to change the price to $160,000 and hold the same amount of value in consumers' eyes.

Going from "free" to "paid" works the same way.

Giving a product away for free is an easy way to confuse the concept of "people really like it" with "people really like it *and* they are willing to pay me for it." People should pay for products that have value and creating a business that ignores this is digging your own grave. Give them a taste, maybe, but if they want the whole entrée (and if you want to stay in business) you had better charge full price.

Recommendation:

- If you must give some part of your product or service away, give them just enough to get them hooked and charge them for every fix thereafter. Giving too much away for free masks the commercial viability of your business.

Summary

With the advent of the Internet and lower-cost marketing methods a lot of new companies have been able to grow and get to market quickly without having to be profitable right away. That's good and bad.

The good part is that companies can get to market quickly and get their products into lots of hands with relatively little cost and time involved.

The bad part is that it's easy to give the product away for free, but hard to charge for it later. Establishing value becomes far more challenging for a young company when they have not set a precedent in the customer's mind.

Startup companies can therefore grow very quickly at the cost of profitability and that's a huge problem. Companies must go to market with business models that put profitability and sustainability at the forefront and use "give it away for free" tactics as a means to an end – not the end.

Final Thoughts

As you can see, going BIG! has a lot more to do with careful planning and execution than it does just "being in the right place at the right time." Although that always helps! *Go BIG!* companies know how to apply the four key principles described in this section in just the right way to address market opportunities.

Frankly, it's extremely hard to pull off all four of these at the same time, but that's why so few companies become the Amazons, Googles, and eBays of the world. But at least that path to getting there is somewhat formulaic – something you can follow.

Thinking big goes beyond just having big ideas or grandiose visions. It's about developing well-thought out strategies for actually implementing those visions. Hopefully you can begin using these four points as a benchmark by which to compare your own strategies.

Growth.

Compress Time

As new market opportunities keep popping up faster, the windows of opportunity seem to be getting smaller and smaller. Startups are learning how to go from "mind to market," or "concept to implementation" in a matter of months, not years.

It doesn't take much time to get a company into the market anymore. For some ideas it doesn't take much more than the creation of a website to get your company ready to start serving customers. A company as big as Yahoo! can get started by two guys in a room with a collection of Web links.

For this reason, your new idea doesn't have a very long shelf life. By the time you write a business plan, find some office space, and begin looking for capital, three competitors could have already snuck up behind you and brought similar products to market.

Startups these days need to learn how to "compress time" in their formative stages so that they can get to market as fast as humanly possible. Many of the old-school rules don't apply anymore. The old idea of opening up shop, hanging out your shingle, and building your company over a few decades just doesn't make sense anymore. Companies don't have years and decades to get to market and grow. They have *months*.

Taking a company from concept to implementation in a matter of months requires a different approach to business formation. This approach forces a company to strip the company's formation down to the barest essentials with a focus on speed over "building infrastructure." *Go BIG* companies are literally compressing the amount of time it takes to build their companies.

Getting a company into market quickly is just the beginning though. Once you're actually "in market" you need to grow as fast as humanly possible just to keep ahead of everyone else. *Go BIG* companies don't just grow over time; they learn to "scale" exponentially. They go from tiny little ideas to major industry powerhouses in a matter of years.

In this section we are going to dig into the challenges that startups face from the moment they conceive an idea until well after they've arrived in the market. We are then going to take a look at what you can do to get your own idea to market quickly and how to "scale" your business to grow as fast as humanly possible.

VideoBlog: our guinea pig

To illustrate the points in this section we're going to take a sample company concept and point out how we can strip it down to the bare essentials to get the company to market as fast as possible and keep it as lean as possible. Then we are going to figure out how to grow it up as fast as possible. It's all about speed and scale.

Our guinea pig sample company will be "VideoBlog," a new service that will allow amateur videographers to upload short video vignettes to our server and allow others to view them. It's like the wildly popular Internet blogging services, but with video on the pages instead of text. We'll make money by charging our content producers to host their videos on our site, providing both a place to upload their videos as well as an audience to view them.

VideoBlog may or may not be a successful company in the end, but what we will focus on in this section is how fast we can get the company to market and how quickly we can scale them to be a big company.

So strap on a helmet, it's time to *Go BIG!*

Chapter 5

Build Backwards

Let me start by showing you the beauty of doing it backwards. No, this isn't the prologue to the Kama Sutra, although we are talking about getting things done from a different angle. It's often helpful to conceive and build your business backwards – envisioning where we want to be in the future and then figuring out how to get there faster.

Starting with the end in mind encourages focus on what we are setting out to accomplish. This in turn makes it easier to eliminate any tasks that won't bring us closer to our goal. Organic growth is interesting, but it's fundamentally unfocused. Chasing random opportunities and figuring it all out as you go can be disastrously slow.

If we plan on getting through our timelines faster we have to be able to understand exactly what those timelines are. Our first exercise will be to lay out exactly what our business would look like over a specific period of time. Once we identify critical milestones, then we can turn our attention toward achieving them faster to compress our timelines.

Define Success

Building the company backwards starts with defining exactly what you are setting out to create. You wouldn't build your dream home without some idea of what the finished product would look like and an undertaking as complex as a startup is no different.

We want to make our definition of success as specific as possible, so we know where the "finish line" is. This definition of success isn't necessarily the finish line. You aren't going to pack up and go home after you reach it. Rather, it's a point where you believe your business will have achieved a significant goal – picked for the express purpose of figuring out how to reach it quickly.

Admittedly, picking this point is more art than science. You want to pick something far enough out that you aren't going through this process every week and something close enough so you can stay in touch with changes in the market.

Here are some important elements of your "finish line."

Be specific. The more detail you provide about your goal the better. Instead of saying "we want to be the leader" try to say explain what that position would require you to have achieved (more customers, more visitors, etc).

Be realistic. We all want to *Go BIG*, but deciding that you want to be the only line of clothing that anyone will ever wear is pretty ridiculous. Look for a goal that you could logically see happening.

Be near term. What you set out to be in the short term and what you evolve to in the longer term could be different. Today you could be the best operating system for personal computers. In the future you might evolve to becoming the world's largest software company. One step at a time.

For the purposes of VideoBlog, we're going to say that we are trying to become the most heavily-trafficked video blogging service with more uploaded videos and a broader selection of content than any other hosted video blogging service.

Notice that we didn't say "we want to be the biggest blog service." That would be a little too broad – it would imply that we want to be number one at text blogging, audio blogging, etc. We focused on one particular market (video blogging) and one particular goal with quantifiable metrics – number of visitors and number of videos.

We also picked a goal that we could reasonably achieve in the next three to five years. Once we got that big, could we evolve to become the next MTV network? Sure, but let's worry about that when we get there. For the time being creating the largest video blogging service would be a nice finish line for us.

At this point we still don't know how *long* it will take to get to our goal, but we at least know what our goal is. Figuring out the timeline is our next step.

Recommendations:

- Pick a goal that your company is setting out to achieve overall. Make it well-defined and quantifiable so you know whether or not you're getting close. Open-ended and amorphous goals won't let you know whether you are getting closer to achieving them any faster.

- Think about this goal like you would think about finding a point on a map. Once you know specifically where you're trying to go, finding the shortest path is a lot easier.

Set your Milestones

Now that we know where we are trying to go, let's figure out how long it will take to get there. The critical milestones for a startup company revolve around getting to market quickly and proving yourself once you're in the market. That's what we're going to focus on here.

I'm not going to suggest that I know exactly what your milestones are but if you're like most startups, they probably look something like this:

1. **Get to market.** Get our product developed and make it available to consumers as quickly as possible. This might include just getting the VideoBlog website up and running and giving people access to our core product.

2. **Get to a "break-even."** Once the product is up and running our next goal would be to get the company to a "break-even" point on expenses. This would put our focus solely on earning cash to keep from going out of business. This might take months. It might take years. But until we get to this point we'll have a hard time staying in business, which is a pretty important goal.

3. **Get majority market share.** This may or may not precede #2. Sometimes a company needs to get majority market share in order to generate enough revenues to become profitable or break even. Regardless, in our business we are going to focus on fiscal issues before trying to drive market share because we really like the idea of paying our bills.

Setting your milestones and knowing what it will take to meet them is important because we are going to spend the rest of our time figuring out how to squeeze them together as tightly as possible.

We also want to use them to focus how we spend our time. We can't address them all at once, so focusing specifically on one milestone is incredibly helpful once we're up and running. You're never going to "get majority market share" if you haven't figured out how to get your product to market yet!

Within each of these major milestones there are smaller milestones that make up the larger goal. For example, we may find that in order to "get to market" we need to first develop a beta version of the software for testing. So "develop and release beta version" becomes one of the milestones within "get to market."

This book isn't long enough to go into the details of every mini-milestone so I'll trust that if you can figure out what the major milestones are, the mini-milestones will become self-evident.

Recommendations:

• Lay out each of your milestones sequentially to map out where your company needs to go from basic inception to the final point of nirvana. (Wherever you defined success, not the rock band.)

• Once you're ready to get moving, stay focused on one milestone at a time. You can't become profitable if you don't have a product to market yet, so don't let the other milestones distract you until you can do something about them.

Wire the Exit

Another important aspect of building backwards is knowing what the "final event" of your startup actually looks like. Investors will often ask a startup company who is seeking funding what their "exit strategy" looks like. An exit strategy is your plan to turn your startup company into some sort of payday for investors through an acquisition or in some cases an IPO.

While we'd all love to believe our company will go public and go on to become an industry stalwart that carries the S&P 500 on its shoulders, let's face it – that rarely happens.

A more likely scenario involves your company being purchased by some larger company, hopefully for a nice, fat profit.

With this in mind, startup companies are putting more emphasis on how to position themselves from the get-go for a financial exit. They do this by figuring who would be in the best position to buy a company with their particular offer and then crafting their product to fit nicely in those companies' portfolios.

Where is the love?

Wiring the exit starts with finding out exactly who your potential suitors might be. For VideoBlog we might create a list something like this:

VideoBlog list of acquirers:

> **Portal Companies (Yahoo!, MSN, AOL)** – These companies would have an interest in VideoBlog because they already have consumers who use complementary services such as photo sharing, email, and instant messenger.

> **Blogging Companies (Blogger, SixApart)** – These companies are an obvious fit because they already have customers who are using blogging services and would likely be interested in the increased functionality of VideoBlog.

Personal Networks (MySpace, Match.com) – These companies rely on a great deal of interaction between people where a video service could enhance the socialization and exchange of ideas.

The list of acquirers can be more than just companies who share the same exact business model. Often companies are acquired because they have a complementary service that enhances a company's business model.

The on-line auction giant eBay purchased payment processor PayPal for $1.5 billion, not because PayPal offered any auctions, but because they had a great payment system that eBay users liked a lot.

Get in where you fit in

(Yes, the title is a Too $hort reference) To understand where you would offer the most value to your potential acquirers, try putting yourself in their shoes. What would an acquiring company stand to gain by purchasing your company that would make that acquisition so worthwhile?

By putting ourselves in the shoes of Match.com, for example, we may realize that having a powerful video display and sharing platform would encourage more of their "would be" members to actually pay for the premium service. Understanding how our service translates into more revenue for a potential acquiring company is what wiring the exit is all about!

Perhaps you have a novel technology that would enhance the experience for the rest of their customers significantly (like PayPal did for eBay). Or perhaps your service offering could be offered to all of their customers right away, creating a new revenue stream that they could not have previously capitalized upon.

There's no one strategy that applies to all companies but if your strategy creates incrementally more value for your acquirer, you're probably on the right path.

Get some metrics

You should also do some homework on each of these companies to learn what types of companies they have acquired in the past and for what reasons. Public companies who have acquired smaller companies are usually required to disclose a fair amount of information about their acquisitions, so these are good places to start.

Specifically you want to know key metrics like how much they paid for these companies and what those companies were generating in revenues before the acquisition. In researching Yahoo! we would find that they acquired companies such as GeoCities, Rocketmail, and eGroups. In each case we can dig deeper to find out what they were acquired for to get a sense for what types of prices these companies are willing to pay.

You'll need these metrics when you go back to investors if you are going to raise capital for your business. They'll want to know what kind of return on their investment to expect based upon how other companies have been valued.

Package it up

Once you understand who has an appetite for buying companies like yours and what they are willing to pay, your next step is to start positioning the company to be acquired.

The best way to do this is to build relationships with your potential acquisition targets (many of them may be competitors in fact) and look to exploit opportunities that they are not taking advantage of yet. Each asset you build that your potential acquirers do not have is one more reason to purchase your company.

Savvy entrepreneurs know that the more complementary they can make their company's offerings to potential acquirers the more likely these acquirers will be to buy their startup versus building the services out themselves.

There's no guarantee that your exit strategy will deliver a big sale for your company. There's a little bit of luck and timing involved in every acquisition. But you can certainly tip the scales in your favor by positioning your company early on as a valuable acquisition candidate – surveying the market of buyers from the start and positioning your company strategically.

Recommendations:

- Start with the exit in mind. The better you understand the needs of the types of companies that could potentially acquire you, the better you can position your company for a possible sale.

- Think about how what you are building today could potentially have value for other companies, and how you could pitch that value into a potential acquisition. As a side note – if it doesn't have value to your customer first, it doesn't really matter if it has value to an acquirer!

Summary

Building backwards, while it may sound somewhat counter-intuitive, is critical in understanding how your business will grow. It's not just about planning for the future, it's also about understanding what you are really setting out to achieve.

Most companies never look past the next year in real, quantifiable terms of growth. Building backwards forces you to lay out the milestones of *exactly* where you want to be in the future so you can figure out the shortest path to that destination.

Companies that are particularly interested in "building it and flipping it" (building fast, selling quickly) should focus on the ideas behind "wiring the exit." Although some startups just go out and building great companies that happen to get acquired, the startups that are more likely to get acquired are those that pay close attention to the marketability of their company as a whole, not just their company's product.

Whatever your long-term preferences, everyone can benefit from spending some time thinking about where they want to be in the long term. As I've always said, it's hard to know whether you're winning the race if you don't know where the finish line is.

Chapter 6

Cut out the Fat

Cutting out the fat in your business plan is really about eliminating the tasks and activities that are not central to increasing the speed and scale of the business. It's also about focusing on what will make or break your business model and leaving everything else on the back burner.

The problem that startup companies often face is that they are easily distracted. They spend so much time "building the company" by creating infrastructure that they lose sight of "growing the company" by adding more customers and revenue.

Cutting out the fat in your model is about stripping away all of the activities that don't directly relate to proving your business model and growing the company. You can't completely avoid building infrastructure but you can change your priorities to focus on growth first.

If it ain't makin' dollars, it ain't makin' sense

If your organization doesn't make money at some point in the near future, you won't be around long enough to worry about much else, so let's start with this one.

It's so easy to get hung up on the details – building the product, talking to partners, meeting with investors, and generally building the company – that you can quickly lose sight of the profit motive for being in business.

While each company has different priorities, they all share the need for revenue to support the business. For this reason your first question for any milestone should be "will this make us money faster?" If the answer is "no," consider moving it down the priority list or eliminating it. The activities that generate cash will keep you around long enough to support the ones that don't.

Stuff that "doesn't make dough"

Building infrastructure. Who cares if you have an HR manual or a neatly crafted org chat if you don't even have any employees? The time you spend writing a "welcome to our company" manual could be better spent calling 10 prospective customers. Worry about building corporate infrastructure when you actually have enough employees for those efforts to even matter.

Buying stuff. Everyone likes shopping for fancy laptops, flashy staplers, and that one cool desk from IKEA but it's not making you money. It's costing you money. All you need is access to a computer and a telephone and you're in business. Spend as little time as possible doing anything else.

Writing strategy. A wise man once said "failing to plan is planning to fail." He was certainly right, but he probably wasn't running a startup company. Don't sit around planning forever. A startup needs to spend more time "doing" and a lot less time writing strategy documents and "thinking about starting."

This line of thinking shouldn't be hard to decipher. As long as you keep asking yourself "is the time I'm spending right now earning the company more money?" (and the answer is always "yes") then you're in good shape.

Recommendations:

- Cash is king. Promote all activities and milestones that will get you to a point where you can generate revenue and earn profit faster.

- Put off building infrastructure as long as possible (hiring accounting staff, writing HR policies, etc.). Generating revenue should be a top priority. Once you have a steady stream of cash coming in, you'll be able to build the infrastructure to support the business.

Does it validate our assumptions?

After you've considered if an activity will make money, the next question should be "does it validate our assumptions?" Some activities may not generate revenue right away but still validate critical assumptions about whether or not your business has a legitimate revenue opportunity.

An assumption in the business model for our video blogging service might be "for every 1,000 visitors to our website, one of them will sign up for our paid service." This is also known as our "conversion rate" and it's a critical assumption for any company.

Startup companies rarely have any operating history so most of their planning is based upon assumptions of what the company *will* do once it's up and running. From there all of the company's projections are based upon those assumptions. The sooner the company can validate those assumptions the sooner management will know whether or not the future forecasts for growth are accurate.

For this reason we will want to do whatever we can to get our website up and running and get some initial customers to the site. We want to test our assumptions quickly so we can begin to form a more realistic strategy for attacking the market.

We may find that in our initial tests we only get one paying customer for every 10,000 visitors. That kind of information can make sweeping changes in our plans to grow. We may need to spend more in marketing than we had originally projected, lower our price point, or expand our list of features. All of these changes can result from validating just one simple assumption.

If we spend lots of time adding additional features when we could have already launched the site and begun validating our assumptions we are slowing our potential growth. The only way we can know for sure that we need additional features is if we determine that our initial assumptions for growth proved to be invalid.

Any activity that keeps you from validating your assumptions more quickly should be cut out of the process. The faster you have answers the better prepared you will be to make changes to your model to improve your efficiency.

Recommendations:

- Pick off your most important assumptions that will make or break your model and try to get to them before anything else. The faster you understand the model, the sooner you can allocate your time properly.

- Even though some activities may not generate revenue, if they help prove whether or not your business model is effective then they may be worthwhile.

Can we live without it?

The difference between what would be "nice to have" and what is "absolutely necessary" in your business can cost you an enormous amount of time and expense. *Go BIG* companies strip down to the bare essentials in every aspect of their businesses. They cut every possible cost and eliminate every activity that the business can live without. Anything that isn't driving the business is dead weight ready to be cast overboard.

If you have a laptop, a chair, a desk, and an Internet connection you have everything you need to be in the video blogging business. No additional infrastructure is necessary. Sure it would be nice to get fancy offices, a great looking business card to impress your friends, and of course a car-load of business stationery and supplies from Staples to help you along. Forget about it! It's all dead weight.

Buying all that crap only costs you time and money. It's not going to make more people want to use your video blogging service, and that's what matters.

It's not just the infrastructure of the business that you can do without (remember "if it ain't makin' dollars it ain't makin' sense!") but some aspects of your business model as well. You can reduce the number of features you create on your product, limit your market to just a domestic region, or skimp on the fancy design of your website in exchange for more function.

For our video blogging service we need to have a website up as soon as possible with the ability to view videos and upload videos. That's it. The faster we get that to market the faster we're adding customers. Some day when we prove that this service makes money and scales we can get around to finding office space, writing a marketing plan, and giving everyone C-level titles. For now our only focus is the business.

Recommendations:

- Take anything and everything that you can possible live without off your "to do" list. If it doesn't involve getting to market faster, proving your assumptions, or generating revenue, dump it!

- Just as a side note, you really *can* live on Ramen Noodles, a dial-up connection, no heat or air conditioning, and a crappy laptop for years. I did it at Blue Diesel for three years and it worked out just fine!

Summary

Go BIG companies understand that if it isn't time spent growing the company or proving the business model, it's time wasted. Startup companies simply cannot afford to waste time, especially in today's business climate when a year can mean the difference between being the next Google and being one of the dozen companies who tried to follow them.

To stay lean and mean you need to remain intensely focused on the few aspects of your business that matter – getting customers and proving the business model.

The ideal *Go BIG* startup would have no overhead of any sort – just a few guys (and gals) in a room working around the clock with a computer, a phone and a case of Red Bull! Anything that isn't driving the ship forward is an anchor holding it back. 'Nuff said.

Chapter 7

Squeeze out the Air

Once you've cut the fat it's time to squeeze the empty air out of your model. You may be focusing on the most critical milestones of your business, but that doesn't necessarily mean that you've found the fastest and most efficient way to get them done.

Squeezing out the air is about taking what's left on your plate (after you've cut out the fat) and compressing it as much as possible so that it gets done even faster.

While there are many places to compress timelines in a business, the three that seem to pop up most often are the timelines associated with sales cycles, marketing launches, and product development. I'll cover each of them individually so you can get a sense for how they can (and should) be compressed.

By all means don't limit yourself to the areas that I've mentioned. In fact, you may have already addressed these areas. The examples here are simply meant to give you a feel for some areas that can be made more efficient. Ideally you'll want to apply this same line of thinking to all aspects of your business.

Sales Cycles

Finding a way to squeeze your sales timelines is crucial in a startup company where the next invoice could translate into your next paycheck. Instead of worrying about how to get by between long sales cycles, let's get those cycles reduced so that the money comes in faster.

Offer less

Sometimes delivering a full-featured product results in needing to ask too much (financially or otherwise) of the customer, causing them to think twice about spending their money or making a purchase commitment.

The hold-up is not driven so much by their lack of interest in your product as the size of commitment you require them to make in one shot. In this case, consider offering less of your product, which may reduce your customer's price barriers and anxiety around making a purchase decision.

At VideoBlog we may find that offering a comprehensive video hosting solution that involves gigabytes of space and tons of available bandwidth requires a great deal of cost on our part, so we need to create a price that reflects this increased cost.

Unfortunately that increased price also causes our potential customers to spend a little more time thinking about our product before they make a decision to buy. We've just instigated a longer sales cycle.

Our solution would then be to create a smaller version of the product that costs us less to deliver and drives the price down to a point where the customer thinks it's a "no-brainer." Voila! Shorter sales cycles.

Recommendations:

- Analyze the drivers behind your sales cycles — what inhibits customer decisions? The faster you break down those barriers the shorter your sales cycles will be. Consider offering a "bite size" version of your product that's easy for the customer to digest.

Create a trial

For the same reasons you would offer less, consider offering a trial. Trials don't require a customer to commit and leaves their options open. The trial allows your customer to get familiar with your product and eases their way past any objections they might have if you just threw a huge price on the table. As I've said, fewer customer objections mean a shorter closing time.

In the case of VideoBlog we may give customers the ability to upload three of their videos to our site for free since this doesn't cost us much and it "pulls" the customer into a purchase decision by creating some commitment to the product.

During this time we may also find that some of their basic objections like "will I understand how to use this?" are addressed quickly and therefore bring them closer to a purchase decision. Most customers will feel much better about your product once they've gotten a chance to play with it.

Recommendations:

- Give your customers something to play with. The more time someone spends with your product the more likely they are to adopt it. Creating a trial allows you to get your product into your customer's hands faster, and that means your adoption begins faster.

Development Timelines

Nothing is more frustrating than having a team that is chomping at the bit to get a new product to market but is mired in endless cycles of product development. While we all want to produce an incredible product, we don't want to wait forever to take it to market.

The faster you put a product out there, the faster a customer can pay for it, and the faster you can reinvest those earnings in growth. Here are a few ideas to consider for shortening your development timelines.

Good enough is good enough

Not everything you create will be a masterpiece, and in most cases it doesn't need to be. You may think that one extra feature is going to make the difference to a customer, but is it worth waiting another two months to get it? Ask yourself, will your customers put your product back on the shelf without that feature or will this prolong your timeline without any meaningful increase in revenue?

For our video blogging service we already agreed that the most basic functionality – the ability to upload and view videos – will suffice. While we can add tons of other features such as the ability to rate the videos, email them to a friend, or save our favorite videos, the basic features of the service are good enough to get us to market.

Every new feature you add costs time, not to mention money. You have to strike a fine balance between what's "good enough" and what's "just too little." You're looking to get the product right up to the point of "good enough" and stop there!

Recommendations:

- The fastest way to crunch your product development timelines is to build less of a product. These days customers expect a product to be evolutionary so you don't have to show everything in your first release. If the core idea of the product is strong, the features will only make it better.

Create a beta version

You don't need to wait until the very end of the product development timeline to ship a portion of your product. Video game developers ship demo versions of their products months before the final product is ready to be released.

This allows them to get the product "out there" early while generating interest and demand for the final release. Look for ways to give the buying public a taste of what's to come so that you can speed their adoption when the final product is available.

You also get the benefit of early feedback about the product. It's hard to predict exactly how the market will react to your product before it's released. Spending too much time building features that you find later will never be appreciated or used is time you can't afford to waste.

We might then create a beta version of our product that just has the most basic features available, with very little time or energy spent on the user interface or any supporting "help" screens. We would then expose this beta version to a small test group to get some initial feedback to see what aspects of the application they love and what aspects they just don't care about.

Recommendations:

- Creating a beta version is not only important to helping market your product, it's also important to get early feedback on the customer response to the product. Look for ways to create a small beta version as soon as possible to help guide your future product development decisions.

Marketing Launches

A well-timed marketing plan can drastically reduce the time it takes to bring in customers. It starts well before the product launches, much like a movie trailer advertising a film that isn't going to come out for another six months. You get an early feel for the level of interest in the product and the feedback allows you to make later marketing efforts more effective.

Most startups only consider their marketing activities as something that you do after they get the product to market. The best way to ensure a product gets ramped up quickly upon launch is to start the marketing machine well before the product ever goes to market.

Start early

You don't need to have the product ready to *talk* about the product. Customers are used to hearing about "upcoming launches" so get in front of them early and prepare them for your product. Explain what it will do and how it will make a difference compared to the current product offers. More importantly, listen to how customers are reacting to your claims. Use this information to shape your product for speedier acceptance when it's released.

We may decide to get the word out early about our upcoming VideoBlog service by joining on-line newsgroups and posting messages about the release, emailing a discussion list with ideas about the product, or even writing a text blog about the development of the product.

Getting the word out to your early adopters is particularly important, since they often have more interest, feedback, and in some cases sympathy for an early-stage product. You're not only building a discussion group, you're also building your initial group of customers.

Recommendation:

- Marketing timelines usually extend farther than they should because they start too late. The earlier you can get your customers buying into your product, the more your overall timelines will feel compressed.

Get pre-orders

Nothing confirms that your marketing is effective and your product is desirable than getting people to commit to a product that's not in their hands yet. Create an opportunity for your customers to pre-order your product, even if that means giving a slight discount. You are now compressing both your marketing timelines as well as your sales cycles!

For our VideoBlog service we may give our "early adopters" a price break for signing up early or before our full feature set is launched. This is also the ultimate test of how much they *really* like the service and whether or not it's worth paying for. While pre-orders do provide the ability to create a little bit of cash flow early, the true value of pre-orders is the affirmation of value to your customers.

Recommendations:

- Finding out whether or not your customers are interested in actually paying for the product is the ultimate test of smart marketing. A product that people feel so good about that they will pay for before its even available has a ton of value.

- I've found that sometimes the process of trying to get pre-orders is a great way to find out how hard its actually going to be to make the sale. Most people will buy a product they like even if they cannot have it today – you do this every time you buy a book on Amazon. Pre-orders allow you to give the sales cycle a trial run, which is always a good thing.

Summary

Squeezing the air out of your business is critical to get to market faster. *Go BIG* companies live by the motto "anything that *can* be done faster, *should* be done faster!"

It's all about taking as many shortcuts as possible. And you have to, because if you can't find a faster way to get your company up and running quickly, your competitors will. Once you are established and growing you can begin to fill in the holes you created along the way. The goal right now is to be around long enough to worry about those holes.

Chapter 8

Identify the Growth Factors

You may recall from the Vision section that one of the four attributes that *Go BIG* companies exude is the ability to "Scale Quickly." Scaling quickly is based upon your ability to locate the growth factors in your business. The growth factors are the aspects of your business which, when tweaked properly, can allow you to scale the business at an exponential rate.

In this chapter we are going to go beyond the theory of growth factors and discuss how to actually implement them in a startup company. Compressing timelines and getting to market quickly is critical, but it's all for nothing if we don't have a plan to grow like mad once the business is launched.

Let's face it, though, not every company is going to grow like Google – that's fine. While I'm using an Internet company to describe how growth factors can play into the expansion of a business, that doesn't mean you need to be an Internet company to grow like one.

As you read this, consider the principles of these factors and how they could be adapted to your own business. If, of course, you are starting an Internet-based company like VideoBlog, then lucky you – I just did some of your homework for you!

It's also important to note that the growth factors described here are just a few that may influence your business. The point isn't that you need to build your business model around all of these points; it's that you need to pinpoint the aspects of your business that will cause you to grow quickly.

Alright, enough caveats. Let's get into the meat of how we are going to grow our little VideoBlog service into an industry behemoth.

Cost of Incremental Sales

Managing the costs of each incremental sale is critical in keeping your expenses from spiraling out of control. It's typical for a company to see its cost of sales steadily increase over time. Once you begin growing you begin hiring more managers, renting more office space, and building more infrastructure. The days of minimal startup costs quickly wane when you start getting big.

All of these costs add to the cost of delivering your product to a customer. Over time the problem companies often experience is that while their product was cost effective (and profitable) to deliver to a few people at first, it became wildly expensive and actually lost money when the company grew.

The key to growth is to push this trend in the other direction – to actually push the cost of incremental sales *down* over time. This will allow us to continue to grow as well as take advantage of economies of scale.

Here are a couple ways in which you can try to force the cost of incremental sales down as you continue to grow:

> **Leverage technology**. Whenever you can add more sales by simply adding more cost-effective technology, you're usually in good shape. That's why a company like VideoBlog has it easy – the business model is *based* upon technology. In our case we can simply

add more servers to service more customers, a process that only has minimal increases in cost.

That's also why many of the fastest growing companies are based upon Internet technology – it's just as cost effective for a website to service 10 customers as it is 10,000.

You don't need to be an Internet-based business to leverage technology, though.   Even movie theatres have leveraged technology to put ticket kiosks in their lobbies.   The ticket kiosks effectively reduce the cost and hassle of staffing someone to service additional customers.

Eliminate people.   No, I don't mean *Terminator*-style. I mean from a productivity standpoint.   If online travel service Expedia had to staff an actual salesperson for every hundred visitors that visited the website their overhead costs would be out of control.

Instead, look for ways to reduce headcount as your company grows, which will effectively keep your incremental sales costs lower. Companies like Craigslist.org are able to service tens of millions of customers with a staff of less than 20 people by simply looking for ways in which technology can solve the problems that would otherwise require people.

Anticipate clutter.   It's a common mistake for startup companies to assume that just because they were able to deliver the product cost-effectively when they were "two guys in a room" that the same would hold true as they grew larger.   Not so.   In fact, most companies become less efficient as they grow and add more "clutter" (a euphemism for "middle management").

This clutter creates increased cost though it doesn't necessarily deliver more products.   While it may be somewhat inevitable, it's only a real problem if you don't anticipate the problem.   Instead, be sure to anticipate the amount of infrastructure you're going to need when you hit key milestones in your growth. Be realistic. If you fail to forecast properly your once-profitable enterprise could spiral out of control very quickly.

These of course are only a few suggestions. The focus here is to think about what costs are likely to escalate as you deliver your product to customer number 10, 10,000, and 10,000,000.

Developing a business model that will keep your costs down while your top-line revenues reach skyward will be the key toward growing quickly.

Recommendations:

- Project your associated costs of sales as your company grows. Do you notice one item that continues to scale at the same rate as revenue growth? That's a good place to start finding ways to reduce that cost to increase your margins.

- Technology seems to be the most popular cure to incremental costs. Ask yourself in every possible case – could this be better handled with an automated process? Is there a cheaper way to get this done?

Speed of Growth

Not only do we need to be concerned about the cost of growing quickly, we also need to be concerned about the speed of our growth as well. *Go BIG* companies can go from zero to $100 million in a few years not only because they have products that people want, but also because they can quickly scale their infrastructure to deliver these products.

Imagine if we had launched our VideoBlog service today and the demand was off the charts. People were signing up left and right – we couldn't take orders fast enough. Good problem to have, right? Not necessarily.

As customer demand grows rapidly we still need to be able to scale up quickly to respond to that customer demand, and that requires not just money, it requires *time*. We need time to hire people to answer support calls, technicians to add more servers and so on. All of these activities, no matter how cost-effectively we can address them, require time.

And if we're caught up in our own underwear trying to solve these problems, our impatient customers are going across the street to our competitor to get the job done.

In order for VideoBlog to *Go BIG*, we're going to have to figure out how to *grow BIG* and do it *fast*.

I often see companies overlook this fact when discussing their ambitious growth plans.   It's easy to add 50 people each quarter in an Excel spreadsheet, but try finding, interviewing, hiring, and training 50 people in three months. It's not easy, and it's certainly not quick.

There are plenty of ways to increase the speed of delivery for your product. Here are just a few:

> **Outsource it.**   Instead of figuring out how to hire people and acquire resources as fast as possible, the alternative is to look for ways to outsource it, at least temporarily.   Anywhere that we can find "plug and play" resources to get the job done immediately without sacrificing the quality of our product delivery is key.
>
> For example, we may decide that bringing up additional servers for our VideoBlog service will cost us too much time, so instead we will find a hosting provider who already has dozens of servers waiting to be utilized. We may decide that instead of staffing a call center we will find an outsourced call center that already has the resources.
>
> The list goes on, but these days outsourcing isn't just about saving *cost*, it's about saving *time*.

Find a Partner. We may also find that partnering with another company can allow us to deliver our product quickly without sacrificing the costs. Just because you're the company facing the customer doesn't necessarily mean you're the company producing the product. Wal-Mart sells thousands of products but relies on their partners to produce them.

Finding partners to fill the gaps in your product offering not only allows you to get to market quickly, but also lets you get up to speed quickly since they may already have the delivery infrastructure you need. Sacrificing some of the profit in each additional sale may be worthwhile if you can service and acquire more customers by doing so.

Change Processes. If you feel you've found an aspect of your business that is resisting your efforts to speed it up, consider changing the process altogether. We may find at our VideoBlog company that it takes a long time to bring additional servers online, yet we need those servers to offer additional capacity to your users.

Instead, we could consider offering *less* capacity to our users unless they actually need it. We could just upgrade customers when and if they ask for additional space. Perhaps the problem isn't that we need more servers, it's that we are giving away too much capacity that our customers don't need.

Sometimes the solution you need to deliver your product quickly and grow faster isn't in the actual delivery, it's in the makeup of the product itself. Try changing up your product a bit to see if the problems still exist with different configurations or options.

You may be reading all of this and think to yourself, "wow, I sure hope to have the type of problem where I just can't service all this new business fast enough!" And you know what? I hope you <u>do</u> have that problem! But I also want you to be ready to deliver a solution when that time comes.

Recommendations:

- Every aspect of your growth takes time in one form or another. Look for ways to reduce the time bringing those aspects of your model to market. Every efficiency you create will speed the growth of the company, no matter how small the efficiency appears to be.

- If finding a partner, outsourcing a process, or changing the process altogether can help get the product to market faster (without sacrificing quality) then it's a winner.

Cost Per Acquisition

If I had to pick one growth factor that I would consider to be the hardest to master, it would be cost per acquisition or CPA.

If you've never heard the term, here's my layman's explanation – CPA is the cost directly associated with acquiring a customer. If you spend $2 in marketing capital to earn $3 in sales, your CPA is $2.

That said I've heard a hundred different definitions of this term, from the cost to acquire a visitor to a website to the entire cost to deliver the product (including production and shipping). Frankly, it doesn't matter which definition you live by, as long as you understand how these metrics can drastically change your business.

The incredible inflating CPA

The reason CPA is so influential in your business is because over time if your CPA goes up and not down, you're headed for trouble.

Here's how our CPA could potentially go **up** over time, causing a real problem for us:

When we first launch our video blogging service, we attract a great number of technophiles and video geeks who love to use the service and tell their friends about it. This word-of-mouth initially keeps our marketing costs low, so for every $100 in revenue we are only spending $20 in marketing costs. Not bad.

But when we try to grow the service and attack larger markets that are less familiar with our application, we find that we no longer have the benefit of cheap word-of-mouth advertising and need to start spending heavily on banner ads and magazine ads.

These items are far more expensive but we need them in order to find a larger audience than what our word-of-mouth marketing can bring in the door. So for every $100 in revenue we end up spending $110 in marketing costs. That's bad.

Down with CPA!

Obviously if we can't contain our cost per acquisition over the long term we are going to grow ourselves right out of business. We need to look for ways in which we can drive our CPA down over time by changing our approach for acquiring customers.

Let's assume that our launch went the same way and we got a strong following of early adopters to the system. But in this case we focused our marketing efforts on allowing our existing users to broadcast the news of their video submissions to as many friends as possible. Effectively we are using our existing customer base to attract more customers. We are amplifying our word-of-mouth efforts.

This approach to growth, as opposed to spending incremental dollars on banner ads and magazine ads will allow us to lower our CPA over time. Assuming we can achieve the same rate of growth, this is the type of effort that we want to strive for in developing this growth factor.

Anything you can do to drive your CPA down over time is going to be extremely helpful. Startup companies often never realize their true CPA in their early years because they haven't had to reach out beyond their core group of early adopters who often find the company themselves, versus needing to be influenced by additional marketing spend.

Creating a model that can force this cost downward will allow you to be more profitable, and also free up additional marketing cash to expand your marketing efforts. Even if your actual cost stays exactly the same (you still spend $30 for every $100 of revenue) you are now reaching a bigger audience through a greater marketing spend, and you're on the right track.

Recommendations:

- Project your marketing spend two to three years beyond your initial launch. What factors contribute to the spend going up or down? Those are the CPA growth factors that you need to spend time influencing.

- The laws of the universe seem to always want to drive your CPA up. Look for deliberate strategies (like using your existing customers to attract more customers) that will force your CPA downward over time.

Market Leverage

Market leverage means that as the service grows the value of your service increases along with it while (hopefully) decreasing the value of a competing service. In the case of our video blogging service we may find that our customers want to upload their videos to the service with the biggest potential viewing audience.

Conversely the viewing audience wants to go to the site that has the greatest number of videos available to watch, and presumably the best selection. The notion here is that in a marketplace economy the biggest market is intrinsically the most valuable market.

Very few companies can claim to have this type of competitive barrier to entry, and those that do (like eBay) tend to completely crush their competitors. Not every market you enter will be able to afford this type of opportunity. For example, if you are creating a new clothing line, the chances that you'll be able to create market leverage that will keep anyone else out of your business is pretty unlikely.

On the other hand, market leverage isn't a benefit that is offered exclusively to marketplaces. Whenever the value of each incremental user of your service creates exponentially more value for everyone else, market leverage is in place.

The telephone is a great example of market leverage in action. The value of the telephone network grows exponentially as more and more people begin to use it. While the telephone network is certainly not a "marketplace", per se, the market leverage effective is certainly in place.

All that said, eBay is still the best example of market leverage, so here it is:

eBay: The Masters of Market Leverage

As you are probably well aware, eBay is the world's largest online auction marketplace. They have created a simple Web-based system to allow everyone in the world to sell the crap out of their closet to someone else who apparently wants it. And they make a lot of money doing it.

But what is more intriguing about eBay is the economic effect of their growth. Let's say you wanted to sell an electric guitar that's been sitting in your closet for the last ten years (yes, your Def Leppard dreams are finally over). Your primary interest is in getting this thing sold.

You hop online and find a dozen different marketplaces like eBay where you can list your guitar for sale. But what you are most concerned about is actually selling the item. It costs just about as much to list the item anywhere you go, so you are looking for the website that has the greatest number of buyers. That would be eBay.

On the flip side there is a buyer out there that is looking for an electric guitar (he is about to start pursuing his own Def Leppard dreams). He is interested in finding the website that has the greatest amount of selection, which will presumably yield the lowest price (also eBay)

Over time, as more buyers and more sellers gravitate toward eBay, the website itself becomes increasingly more valuable based upon the fact that it is snowballing into the biggest and best option for both buyers and sellers.

www.ebay.com

Realizing that being the biggest market will allow us to create market leverage against our competitors, we will want a strategy in place that puts lots of influence on this growth factor.

We may decide that we will forgo a certain amount of revenue in exchange for acquiring more customers and therefore more content. So we may influence this factor by offering video bloggers a small amount of space for free, compared to our competition that charges a fee for any use.

The Market Leverage of Swapalease.com

Understanding the value of market leverage is extremely important in a scalable business because it impacts a great deal of your strategy. At Swapalease.com we realized that if we were the biggest leasing marketplace we would attract the greatest number of buyers *and* sellers, because both audiences had a vested interest in using the biggest marketplace.

If you wanted to sell your lease, certainly you would want to list with the marketplace that had the biggest audience of potential buyers. And if you wanted to find a lease to assume, certainly you would want the biggest possible selection of car leases to choose from.

For this reason we spent all of our time and efforts trying to build the size of the marketplace first, forgoing a certain amount of revenue opportunities in the early years. The gamble paid off though, and Swapalease.com became the world's largest marketplace for auto leases. Now when someone wants to list their vehicle, Swapalease.com is quantifiably the best place to do it because we offer the greatest potential opportunity to find a buyer.

Finding market leverage in your own model often comes down to figuring out why creating a critical mass of customers will make your product more effective than your competitors'. Often a service with a large critical mass offers more selection, more quality, and more opportunity than a smaller service offering the same product.

Recommendations:

- Look for ways to influence customer behavior so that adopting your product provides inherently more value to the customer than adopting a competitor's. If being the larger fish creates more value to a customer than being the smaller fish, focus all of your efforts on creating that critical mass and market leverage to achieve this position.

- Most startups sacrifice revenues for customers in order to achieve critical mass quickly. The most popular "get big quickly" strategy seems to be "give it away." Beware that while giving your product away may be a growth strategy, it's certainly not a revenue strategy.

Final Thoughts

You can't *Go BIG* if you don't plan to grow *BIG*! Having big visions and big dreams means nothing without a strategy to make it happen. As you can see from our discussion in this chapter, companies that plan on going from zero to $100 million or even zero to $1 million as quickly as possible need to have a strategy to get there.

There's certainly no magic formula to making it happen every time. What I've outlined here are just the basics to spur you to think in terms of growing big and fast. Your own mileage may vary.

I can tell you first hand that what I've found to work best is to set a course for big growth and to keep making adjustments along the way. No one plans for "Google growth" on paper and just executes from the same playbook they devised on day one. You need to keep testing your assumptions and making changes with an eye on fast growth the entire time.

I'm a big fan of simply pointing toward the direction you want to go and running in that direction. You're going to hit hurdles – you can't plan around all of them. But the clock is ticking so if you intend on getting to where you want to be quickly, you need to just get started. We have less time than ever to get our ideas to market.

Marketing.

Act like Number One

Before each *Go BIG* company was an industry behemoth they were two guys in a room like everyone else. Yet *Go BIG* companies consistently appear to be Number One in their respective markets from day one.

What you'll find is that these Number One positions have very little to do with the actual size or growth of the company (at least initially). They are about the intelligent positioning of a company to be perceived as a leader, or said differently *as the winner before the race has begun.*

In fact most of these companies really are just two guys in a room. However they are able to position themselves as leading companies to attract the type of attention and credibility that a Number One company deserves. This section is about how these *Go BIG* companies act like Number One from day one.

Getting Noticed and Getting Selected

Marketing your company really comes down to two basic concepts – getting *noticed* and getting *selected*. It's no good to have one without the other.

It all starts with getting noticed which means standing out from the crowd. In every market there is so much noise among competitors and so many forms of media that getting noticed is harder than ever.

Yet getting noticed is only half of the equation – you still need to get *selected*. This means creating an air of credibility that gives people the confidence to say "yes" to your product over your competitors'. You want people to believe that making the decision to buy your services is the right one.

Unfortunately customers have so many choices in the market that it's difficult to evaluate them all. This is where *Go BIG* companies do things differently. *Go BIG* companies know that most customers buy based upon their *perceptions* of what is the most valuable product and can only make decisions based upon what they can perceive to be the best.

Perception is a powerful ally to companies who understand how to translate perceptions into profits. Somewhere in the distance I can hear one of the Creative Directors from one of the ad agencies I worked at saying "this is called *branding*".

Clutter and Credibility

The best way to cut through the clutter and create an air of credibility at the same time is to establish a Number One position. A Number One position stands out from the crowd. It's a winner. It rises above the rest.

When making a product selection, consumers associate Number One with a wise decision that has earned the credibility associated with being the "leader in its class." That means that if you can get to the customer first (get noticed) and quickly convince the customer that you are the best decision (get selected) then you win the customer before your competitor does.

With so much attention and pressure to be Number One, a startup needs to figure out how to attain that status quickly and hold onto it. In this section we are going to talk about how critical it is to be Number One, how *Go BIG* companies think and act like Number One, and how you can create a Number One position for yourself today.

Number Two is Inferior

The problem with being Number Two (or three, or four, or fifty) is that the world feels there must be a reason that you're not Number One. Number Two is inherently the whipping boy for Number One. In order for Number One to have the status that they do, Number Two must have done something wrong.

It's a popular marketing tactic to expose the wounds of Number Two in order to convince consumers that Number One avoids that fatal flaw. The second-guessing that gets built into Number Two creates an instant chasm between the credibility of Number One and Number Two.

You've got enough work ahead of you to build your brand and convince customers to buy – the last thing you need is another hurdle to overcome with your credibility!

People Perceive Anything Less Than Number One as a Loser

When the Stanley Cup is over and the losing team skates off the ice, you don't see people getting all excited about the fact that they came in second. The notion is that they could have been Number One, they failed, and now they are in their rightful place as Number Two. Or said less diplomatically, they are the losers. You can't afford to be perceived as the loser.

As a side note, if you are perceived as the "loser", you can always brand yourself as the "underdog". While it's basically just a shell game of titles, it can also be used as a strategy to help build support for your brand. Unless of course, you really are a loser in which case you can forget I suggested it.

Number One Cuts Through the Clutter

Cutting through the clutter of marketing messages for a startup company with no existing brand equity is a big challenge. There are so many people with so many products all shouting at the top of their lungs that getting your message heard seems nearly impossible.

What *Go BIG* companies do well is position themselves in a way that, regardless of all the noise around them, gets their messages heard. This is because they know how to position their messages as being *more important* than all the others.

Imagine if I were a stock broker cold calling to convince you to invest with my firm. I told you I had an interesting opportunity you needed to hear. You would probably hang up the phone before I finished my first sentence. That's because my message didn't resonate with you. I didn't differentiate myself from all the other clutter you've been hearing.

Now let's try that again, but this time I start by saying that I'm the energy industry's most highly-rated investor and I had an opportunity that I wanted to discuss with you. Now I might have your attention. My leading status ("most highly rated") has created a small window for me to speak just a little bit longer and get my credibility across.

Getting that moment of attention is exactly what your company needs to get its foot in the door. Think of your Number One position as a VIP card that allows you to get past the bouncer at the door. Once you're in the door, now you need to make the sale.

Number One Has Credibility

Your Number One status not only gets you in the door, it also helps you make the sale. There is an implied reasoning for a Number One status – that the person, product, or company must have beaten out everyone else in order to earn that status. Clearly if you were awarded a "winning" status you must have met all the criteria of a winner.

Number One implies credibility. For a startup that has very little traction in the marketplace, credibility is vital to its success.

Let's forget that people rarely take the time to figure out *who* defined those criteria or *why* they were important to begin with. No one questions a winner. The loser, however, instantly carries with it the question of "why didn't you become Number One? You must have made a mistake." It would seem that all the benefits of being Number One carry an exponential downside as Number Two.

When you combine the ability of Number One to cut through the clutter with the ability of Number One to help make the sale, you start to open up doors with all of your important constituents – customers, investors, employees, and the media. Let's take a look at how each group is inspired by your status and how having a Number One position makes you far more successful with these groups.

Customers Buy Number One

Customers have more product choices than ever before. With so many choices it doesn't make sense to settle for inferior or second-rate products.

For this reason every product clamors to a Number One position to be the easy choice for consumers.

Customers want to make decisions that make them feel good. Buying Number One makes them feel like they've gotten "the best", and that's a rewarding feeling especially if the cost difference is negligible.

Creating a Number One position reinforces the customer's sense that they made the right decision. The more comfortable the customer feels with your Number One status, the lower the barrier to accepting your product as their choice.

Investors bet on Number One

This shouldn't be hard to figure out. Imagine you've got $1,000 to invest in the stock market in two different companies. Company A is the market leader and Company B is the market follower.

Immediately you perceive Company A to be the safer bet. Maybe Company B has a lot of potential, but by being the market follower you instantly perceive them to be more of a gamble. Your own company works the same way when outside capital is looking at your deal. Being Number One in your space gives investors the sense that you are a safer bet.

Anything you can do to convince investors that you are the best horse to bet on is a positive. What investors are constantly looking for is that one investment that is about to take off with as little risk associated as possible. Being Number One suggests that you have already proven your leadership position, now it's just a matter of how big you can get.

Top Talent Wants to Work for Number One

Just like an investor, top talent that comes to work for your company is considering the return on their investment of time and expertise. A top company can provide the opportunity that a lesser company cannot. That company can provide not only financial upside but the prestige of working for the leader in a given space.

Getting a job offer from a market-leading company is not only a great opportunity; it's an affirmation of the skills and credibility of the candidate. It's no surprise that the best quarterbacks go to the best colleges and the best attorneys go to the best law firms. They want to go where they are going to be in good company.

Your top talent wants to work for the winning team as well, and nothing says "winning team" like a Number One position. You can use your leading status to attract and retain people to your company. It's a powerful recruiting tool.

The Media Showers Number One

The media can be a powerful ally of any company creating both exposure and credibility to the masses. But the media isn't particularly hard to understand – they cover stories that will get people to read magazines, tune in their TV, and jump on their homepage.

What people want to hear about are the outstanding organizations – the Number One players – in their respective categories that trounce everyone else. Number One is newsworthy. Everyone wants to know what its like to be on top, to be successful, to be dominant. No one cares what Number

Five is thinking.   They didn't beat everyone else out, so they're not newsworthy.

If you're not sure about how much the media loves Number One, think about this – we all know Bill Gates is the world's richest man. We know that because the media tells us all the time. They are infatuated with his Number One status. Well then, can you tell me who the third richest man is? I'll give you a hint – he also started Microsoft.

Most people can't tell you who Number Two and Number Three are because the media gives them no attention. With such a limited amount of space in the media, they can only focus on the players that define their category. And guess what? They are at the Number One spots.

You Need to be Number One NOW

With all the benefits your Number One status affords, you absolutely need to get there as quickly as humanly possible. What we're talking about is understanding how vital Number One is to your success and how being anything less is a huge disadvantage.

Now comes the hard part – actually becoming Number One. We already recognize that the sooner we can get there the better off we will be. *Go BIG* companies know that becoming Number One means taking control of their respective markets and gaining all the attention and credibility of their constituents.

So let's figure out how to get there.

Chapter 9

Think Like Number One

Before you can begin acting like Number One you need to begin thinking like Number One. *Go BIG*! companies think way beyond just beating their direct competitor down the block. They think in terms of dominating their entire market space and controlling the destiny of their respective industries. This thought process is what leads to becoming Number One.

Thinking like Number One isn't just a matter of being optimistic, it's a strategy toward outfoxing your competition completely. Thinking like Number One means challenging yourself and your company to take a leadership position, regardless of where your company may stand in its market space today.

In this chapter I'm going to spend a lot of time discussing the concept of thinking like Number One from the standpoint of a tiny company. That's because most companies in their formative stages tend to acquire a bit of an inferiority complex about their size.

Just remember that every *Go BIG* company started off as just a tiny little startup, but that didn't keep them from thinking BIG!

Size Doesn't Matter

Chances are you aren't going to instantly be the "biggest" in your space from a size standpoint. That's OK. Great products don't come solely from big companies. They come from smart companies who know how to take advantage of market opportunities quickly and extract the maximum amount of value from them.

Your customer may want to buy a product from a leading company, but they don't necessarily care that you are the "largest" in a physical sense. When you get right down to it, most customers will have no idea how big your company is physically. They are going to judge your relative size based upon how well you present your product.

Getting past this notion of "we have to be a big company in order to be a Number One company" is critical. At the very least it could take decades to organically grow to be a physically big company and you don't have that much time!

These days innovation and speed, not size, are the weapons of choice. More market leading companies are weighing in with Number One market positions at a fraction of the size of their larger competitors. Think of how Google's 5,000 employees are running circles around Microsoft's 60,000 employees in the race for online search dominance. It's their speed, not their size that gives them the edge to be Number One.

It's also something you can't quantify – they have big kahoons or <insert inappropriate expletive of choice here>! Thinking like Number One and going up against a company like Microsoft takes a bit of swagger that young *Go BIG* companies are known for.

One of my favorite recent examples of this type of swagger came from Skype, the voice-over-IP telephony company that just went straight at the throats of the biggest goliaths of all time – the telephone titans.

Skype: The New Age David and Goliath

If you want a real David and Goliath story in today's terms, look no further than the Internet telephony company Skype. Founded by the same folks who brought us Kazaa, the popular file-sharing software that operated like Napster, Skype allows you to make calls to your friends and colleagues over the Internet as opposed to using traditional telephony providers.

Phone companies traditionally made their fortunes by charging users fees to make long-distance phone calls. Using Skype, however, customers could avoid long-distance charges altogether by placing their calls through the Skype network, effectively using the entire Internet as their phone line.

Skype thought like Go BIG companies do – like Number One. Instead of worrying about the size of their larger competitors they went at them head on. Skype allowed its customers to download a free version of its software that would enable them to place calls through its network. Within just twenty-four months the company registered over 100 million downloads of its software!

Skype knew that they could move faster without the constraints of big telecom companies. They could leverage the new "free" infrastructure of the Internet to create a much cheaper alternative to traditional long-distance companies. By the time the traditional companies could even respond to what was happening in the marketplace, Skype had over 23 million customers using its service.

www.skype.com

If anyone knew how to *Go BIG* it was Skype. The company was sold to auction giant eBay for a whopping $2.6 billion in cash less than three years from its inception.

Skype is a legendary example of how a small company can become a market leader without having to be "big." Size doesn't matter to *Go BIG* companies, and it doesn't constrain their thinking.

No one cared that Skype was a physically a "small" company. Twenty-eight million users seemed to overlook this fact altogether. What people really cared about was the fact the company could deliver a Number One product that made their lives easier (and cheaper).

When it comes to thinking like Number One, think in terms of what you can accomplish, not in terms of your relative size. The size you are today is an instance in time, not a limit to your potential.

Recommendations:

- Take the view of your customer. List all of the reasons they would not buy your product based upon how many employees you have, how big your offices are, or your gross sales.

- Browse through the company profiles of some of your favorite new companies like Skype, Google and MySpace and compare the size of their companies (employees, locations, etc.) to that of their old-world competitors.

Set a New Standard

While most companies think in terms of how to "improve the norm," *Go BIG* companies break the norm entirely by setting their own standards. The nice thing about setting your own standard is that you create the new yardstick that your competitors are measured against.

As a way of thinking, setting a new standard means approaching problems with the question – "what *should* be done in the marketplace?" – with no regard for what is being done in the marketplace today.

The standards of "how things are done today" are often predicated on historic patterns of behavior. In order to break the mold, *Go BIG* companies start without a mold altogether. They attack the problem from a fresh perspective that allows them to see the problem without the baggage of existing patterns.

You've seen this pattern of innovation emerge again and again. Priceline.com determined that the traditional model of selling airline tickets was flawed. There was a price point that people were willing to pay to fly somewhere, although that price point didn't always match up with what airlines were willing to charge.

Priceline.com took a fresh approach to this problem. Instead of letting the airlines set the fares for their tickets they let consumers suggest the price and allowed airlines to compete for their business. They changed the model by ignoring the standard.

Priceline.com is just one example of a *Go BIG* company that profited greatly from taking a fresh approach. NetFlix is probably one of the best known *Go BIG* companies to completely re-engineer a very tried and true system – the movie rental business. In the process they set a new standard other industry stalwarts would have to follow.

NetFlix: The New Standard in Rentals

NetFlix practically invented the market for online mail-order DVD rentals back in 1998. In just a few short years the company became synonymous with online DVD rentals even though the market for renting movies had been around for decades.

NetFlix thought like a Go BIG company does. As the story goes, Reed Hastings, the CEO of NetFlix, was tired of paying late fees to video rental chains like Blockbuster. So he found a way to change the standard. Instead of renting movies for a fixed period of time and paying late charges if you held them for too long, NetFlix allowed you to keep your movies for as long as you liked.

Thus, NetFlix was born out of the simple notion that "paying late fees really sucks" and there has to be a better way to do business. NetFlix allows users to keep a set number of movies at home for as long as they like for a monthly fee.

The "rent for as long as you like" model was wildly popular with NetFlix customers (myself included) who were quite eager to never pay another late fee. In the process the company actually forced industry behemoth Blockbuster to abandon its late fee structure altogether.

NetFlix set a new standard for the movie rental business and frankly did the world a favor in the process. Thanks!

www.netflix.com

NetFlix is a great example of how a *Go BIG* company acts like Number One by setting their own standard for others to follow. Over time what was once "best in class" often becomes "second class" to a more innovative process or product.

Take a look at your own market. Are the methods your competition uses the best or are they simply inheriting the "way it always has been?" The best way to think like Number One is to forget about the way things have been done in the past and concentrate on how they should be done in the future.

Recommendation:

- Take a look at your new product idea or business plan and ask yourself "how much of this business model was driven from how things are done today?" Try approaching your solution with this question: "If no one had ever done this before, how would I solve this problem from scratch?"

Summary

Thinking like Number One goes way beyond just being confident about your product or service. It's about defining what the leadership position should be and taking that position. What I love about *Go BIG* companies is how well they assume those roles, even when the company is fresh out of the box.

It probably goes without saying, but thinking like Number One is a mind set that starts with the leadership of the organization and is ingrained in the culture of the company. It's not enough to simply say "we should think like Number One." You need to live it and breathe it every day in everything that you do.

Chapter 10

Make Yourself Number One

With all this talk about how important it is to be Number One and how to get in the mindset of thinking like Number One, you may still be saying to yourself "that's great Wil, but I'm Number Fifty in my market category. How does this help me?"

The answer is to make yourself Number One. Don't worry! It's easier than you think.

Creating a Number One brand or market position has a lot less to do with actually growing a company than it does *positioning* a company. When I say that GM is a Number One company you may conjure up a list in your mind that ranks companies by gross revenues or number of cars produced.

But that Number One position, while it sounds like a reward for being a "big company" is actually just an arbitrary metric that someone used in order to rank companies. Positioning your company means rallying around the metrics that not only suit your company best, but mean the most to your customer.

Now I'm going to show you how to become Number One in just one chapter. Hopefully this is worth the price you paid for this book!

Create a New Category

In *The 22 Immutable Laws of Marketing,* Al Ries wrote one of the smartest things I had ever read. "If you aren't Number One in your category today, invent a **new** category!" Everyone is Number One at something; the trick is to determine what Number One is going to be for you.

The first thing you need to understand is that a Number One status is based upon a specific set of criteria. Many companies fall into the trap of thinking that the most commonly agreed-upon criteria for ranking companies must be the criteria they judge themselves by.

Perhaps companies in your industry are ranked by sales volume, head count, or the size of their inventory. No matter what the criteria, the trick is not to buy into the hype, especially since it doesn't suit you. Your job is to define a new set of ranking criteria that holds you at the top of the list.

Before you get some sort of complex about whether it's "fair" to position yourself in a certain manner, consider the fact that whomever has set the ranking criteria and is benefiting by it has not interest in helping you. The worst thing you can possibly do for your company is to accept the fact that another set of criteria (that works against you) is your best option.

Let's go back to the NetFlix example I just used. NetFlix thought like Number One, and therefore decided that if anyone was going to be Number One, it was going to be them. They took this position by simply creating a category that suited them best (and just happened to be the basis for their entire business model) and claimed the Number one spot.

Let me walk you through the exercise of creating a Number One company, just like we did with Swapalease.com.

Swapalease: Number One Overnight

Swapalease.com has always been a Number One company. The only thing that has changed over time is what we have been Number One at. Swapalease.com makes its money when customers who want to get out of a car lease pay to run an ad on the website. Therefore the website that appears most likely to find a buyer for their lease will be the website that most customers will place ads on. We needed to be perceived as Number One.

The problem was that we just started out, so being Number One would seem like a bit of a farce. We certainly weren't as big as some of the major online automotive destinations like Autobytel.com and Edmunds.com. And we didn't have the offline presence of popular publications like Auto Trader or the Dupont Registry.

What we did have, however, was a really specific product – lease transfers. While other sites had lots of traffic and lots of listings, they didn't focus specifically on listings that involved the transfer of an automotive lease. So we began by creating a new category – online lease transfer – and assigning ourselves the rank of Number One.

The funny thing is that we were only Number One in this space because we were the only people *in* this space! But the positioning allowed us to boast an impressive tagline to prospective customers – "America's Largest Online Automotive Lease Transfer Marketplace".

While we were certainly America's largest lease transfer marketplace, we were also the only lease transfer marketplace anywhere! The tag line definitely helped, though, as we soon became known by partners, customers, and even the media as the market leader in a category we completely made up.

The Swapalease.com story illustrates the fact that creating your Number One position is more a matter of being creative than anything else. Over time you can refine your position to be more specific to the interests of your customers ("the most trusted," "the most effective") or to celebrate your elevated status over time ("the city's largest," "the world's largest").

As Swapalease.com grew we modified our positioning accordingly. We eventually swapped out "America's Largest" to "The World's Largest" (that sounds pretty big!). We also dropped some of the extraneous tags such as "online" and "transfer." We soon became known as the "world's largest auto leasing marketplace."

A Number One position, even in a tiny category, is more valuable to most people than a number ten position in a larger category. People often attribute a Number One position as having more value. Conversely a number two (or twenty) position often suggests that you could have done something better to be Number One. It implies you're missing something.

Creating your own category isn't hard to do. Just about anyone can subdivide their market category into a piece that leaves them at the top of the stack. Now all of the sudden you've gone from "struggling startup" to "category killer." Not bad for ten minutes worth of work!

Recommendations:

- Write down a list of everything you are Number One at when compared to your competition. This is your starting point for differentiation in the marketplace.

- Create a new category for your product that puts you in the Number One position. Then promote the benefits of that category versus others.

Make Number One Meaningful

Creating a Number One position by simply creating a new market category is only useful if your customer actually cares about that category. If Swapalease.com is the world's largest auto leasing marketplace in London that doesn't mean much to me if I live in Los Angeles.

In order to make Number One effective, you need to make Number One meaningful to your audience. Being Number One is incredibly powerful if your audience can appreciate what you are Number One at. So perhaps the first step, before you start subdividing your existing market categories, is to figure out what your audience really cares about.

While GM may be repeatedly cited in the media as the "largest auto maker," does it really matter to their customers? Imagine if I were sitting with you at a car lot and told you that for the same price you could have a BMW or a Chevy (a GM brand), which one would you pick?

I'd pick the BMW because frankly I don't care about how many cars GM sells. I would pick the BMW because what's important to me is that they are Number One in the categories that matter to me – style, luxury, and performance. If GM sells 5 times as many cars next year it won't make them any more valuable to me.

Your Number One status really hits home when it's tied to a meaningful position that truly causes customers to buy. At Swapalease.com we promoted ourselves as the world's largest because it implies that we have more customers who have decided to list with our service over any other leasing marketplace.

However if we really wanted to drive the brand position home we could say "We are the fastest option for getting out of your lease." In this case we would be betting that our customers appreciate the fact that we get customers out of their leasing obligations faster than anyone else. It would also imply that we think getting customers out of their leases quickly is incredibly important to them.

Of course this only works if you really *are* the fastest, or the cheapest, or the most effective. Sometimes it's important to append a categorical definition to your claim in order to make it stand out as the leading product or service. For example, you may not sell the cheapest car on the road, but you may sell the cheapest *luxury* car on the road. You get the idea.

Here are some areas that I find are most likely to help companies become Number One in more meaningful categories:

> **Most Effective**. If efficacy is the driving force behind the product, then positioning behind this attribute is golden. If I have the flu I'm a lot less concerned with "the most popular flu relief" than I am with the "fastest-acting flu relief." I want fast results to my pain, not a vote in a popularity contest.

> **Most Dedicated**. Whatever the particular interest of your customer, knowing that you are dedicated to this specific attribute will resonate well with them. If I want to differentiate my flu medicine I would try to rally around a particular symptom that I thought customers would appreciate. For example "the only flu medication dedicated to relieving scratchy eyes."

> **Most Reliable.** In cases where safety or dependability outweighs other claims, most reliable says a lot. We may not be the largest towing service in town, but if we are the most reliable towing service we're a lot more likely to get a phone call from customers!

These are just some suggestions, but you can see how diving into particular needs can help turn a number ten position into a Number One position in the minds of your customers very quickly.

Recommendations:

- Write down a list of the key attributes of your product that you believe influence whether or not a customer buys your product. Are you Number One in one of those? If so, consider leading with that attribute as one of your benefits.

- People love charts and lists. Wherever possible, publish or present a list of the "top ten" people in your newly invented category with your name at the top. For some reason people confer an inordinate amount of value on lists, especially when your name is at the top!

Make Big Bad

Another way to help position you as a Number One company is to actually turn the tables on your largest competitors. Being the "biggest" is not always a good thing. If you are the small player in your space you may find that customers aren't served best by big companies, they are served best by *smart* companies, or more *customer-focused* companies. Turning the tables and using the size of your competitors as a weapon against them is not only powerful, it's kind of fun.

I know this technique works because I've had it done to me when I was working for a small company (inChord) that became a very large company. You would think that the big guy always has his way, but in fact that's rarely the case. With growth comes a whole new set of problems, and holding on to your customers is actually one of the most challenging problems of them all.

Growing in size, shrinking in value

At inChord, a large advertising agency where I was an officer, we grew at an alarming rate. In four years we went from a tiny little agency with $8 million in total revenues to big damn agency with $100 million in revenues.

When we were a smaller agency we had worked with a great client who I'll call LittleCorp, who loved that we were small enough that they owned all of our attention.

As our beloved agency grew quickly, so did our staff and our commitments. Over a short period of time LittleCorp was no longer an "agency changing client," meaning their share of our billings shrunk to 5% of our total revenues.

Our growth meant that we were capable of delivering far more value to LittleCorp, at roughly the same price. We could bring in dozens of experts and provide ground support for their advertising needs throughout the world.

And while all of that sounded like a great idea to us, LittleCorp hated it. LittleCorp didn't want a big honking agency that had lots of Vice Presidents and worldwide offices. They wanted an agency that was at their beck and call. They wanted to be Number One in our eyes. While we rocketed up the charts of Ad Age's list of fastest growing agencies, we plummeted on LittleCorp's list of "things we care about."

In the end LittleCorp fired us for being "too big."

www.inchord.com

It's true. As we grew we became less focused on LittleCorp and more focused on our larger, higher-paying clients. What they created was an opportunity for the next inChord to swoop in and steal LittleCorp. And that's what "making big, bad" is all about – using the lack of focus of bigger companies as a weapon against them.

Most companies, as they grow larger, inherently lose focus in a few areas. Customer service is a popular one but there are certainly others. At inChord we grew at a phenomenal rate, and along the way we lost a lot of key benefits that our clients appreciated. Here are just a few:

> **Attention.** When LittleCorp was our only customer they got VIP treatment all the time. It's not just about inflating the egos of the client (OK, yes it is) it's also about convincing them that you are giving their business as much attention as you would give your own. Big companies quickly lose this asset because they become distracted by so many customers. While this is great news for the big company, it's horrible news for the customer.

> **Personality.** Big companies often shed their initial personality for a "corporate, grown-up look." While that might impress investors in an IPO, it gives customers the sense that they are no longer working with people, but instead are working with a vendor. Our clients at inChord didn't want a corporate greeting card from Wil Schroter. They wanted a phone call and some of his lame jokes.

> **Focus.** When LittleCorp hired us they liked the fact that we did one thing really well – marketing. But over time we got into public relations, media planning, and even speakers bureaus. While that's all well and good, it distracted us from the focus that made us a great agency – marketing. Adding more features doesn't necessarily improve what was one the core benefit.

Again, the list goes on. I almost wished I could have been in the pitch against us when trying to win LittleCorp's ad business away from inChord. I would have never had to even mention how many employees we had or the size of our annual billings. All I would have had to do to be Number One in the eyes of LittleCorp is be the best at giving them attention, personality, and focus. That's what they were really buying.

Turning the tables on the big boys is a matter of finding those pain points in the eyes of your existing customers and using them to your advantage. It's also important to keep in mind that your own company is subject to these same consequences as you grow. For the time being, however, you can take heart in knowing you are on the right side of the equation.

Recommendation:

- Look for all the ways in which the size of your larger competitors creates a problem for consumers and begin building the foundation for your message there. The bigger a company appears to be the less focused on an individual they tend to become. And at the end of the day it's an individual who is consuming your product.

Summary

Creating a Number One position is more about the positioning of your product than it is the size of your company or your annual revenues. What is most important is aligning the interests of your customers with the Number One attributes of your product. Rarely does the physical size of a company relate to the benefit to consumers.

If you can find a meaningful niche to dominate, especially if you are just getting started, you will have created a very powerful weapon to use against your competitors large and small. The trick is knowing where to place your bets.

Chapter 11

Market Like Number One

"Woo-hoo! I'm Number One! Now what?"

Great, you've just promoted yourself from "aspiring startup" to "industry leader." Not bad for ten minutes worth of effort. Now let's talk about what to do with your newly-elevated status.

Positioning your company in the hearts and minds of your audience is just the start. Actually executing on that brand promise is the hard part. In this chapter we are going to talk about what *Go BIG* companies do to reinforce their Number One position in the marketplace.

Spread the Seed

Your Number One status should not exactly be kept a secret. Announce your Number One status on every piece of sales and marketing collateral you produce. Get used to giving your elevator pitch with the opening line "we are the *fastest growing* bookseller in the Midwest" at every chance you get.

It's not enough to include your tagline in just your printed materials. Every touch point that you have with your customers should include some reference that re-affirms your Number One status. It should be in your PowerPoint presentations, at the footer of your email, and on the receipts that your customers take home.

In addition to leveraging your existing touch points, be sure to create some new ones. Issue press releases reminding people that you are Number One, consult with the media to talk about how your product has risen to a Number One status, and ask your customers to provide testimonials to their friends about your Number One status.

As we discussed earlier, Number One companies start spreading the seed about their Number One status as early as possible. Take a look at how NetFlix positioned itself when they started and how they positioned themselves when they became a multi-billion dollar company. They spread the seed as a Number One company the entire time.

NetFlix Press Release 1998
(Source: NetFlix.com)

> With the <u>world's largest</u> selection of DVD movies, NetFlix, Inc. rents and sells DVD movies to owners of DVD video players and DVD-ROM equipped PCs at its Internet store, www.netflix.com.

NetFlix Press Release 2005
(Source: NetFlix.com)

> NetFlix (Nasdaq: NFLX) is the <u>world's largest</u> online movie rental service, providing more than 3.5 million subscribers access to over 50,000 DVD titles.

Every possible message that comes out of your organization should be blessed with your Number One status. Whenever someone would ask about Swapalease.com, we always responded with "Swapalease.com is the world's largest leasing exchange where you can transfer your leasing obligation to someone else." We baked our leading status into the actual description of who we are as a company. Over time the two became synonymous.

Recommendations:

- Make a list of every possible touch point that you have with your customer. Does every message reinforce your leadership status?

- Bake your Number One position into your marketing tagline or even the basic description of your company.

Use Number One to Open Doors

Think of being Number One like being a celebrity. Your superstar status allows you to get into places and talk to people that the average Joe can't get to. That's because companies in Number One positions have more bravado than everyone else. Their confidence in knowing they *should* be on the other side of the velvet rope is what gets them on the other side of the velvet rope. Use your elevated status to get the types of introductions you need to investors, partners, and customers.

Don't call investors and let them know you are yet another online bookstore. That won't get you past the secretary. Call and let them know who you really are – the fastest growing online bookstore in the Midwest. Nothing guarantees they will take your call, but you can be guaranteed to get hung up on if you don't start acting like the Number One player that you are!

Among customers you want to use your Number One status to help close sales. Customers want to buy from companies that make them comfortable. Assure them that the reason you are Number One is because you do what you do better than anyone. Companies with Number One products know their products are the best and act like it. That's what helps close deals and incidentally that's what makes them Number One.

Recommendations:

- Use your Number One status like a VIP pass at every possible door. Remember that if you don't walk into the room with the confidence of being Number One then no one else is going to provide that credit for you.

- Use your Number One status to help close deals. People want to buy the best (assuming the price is right) and what you are representing needs to be just that – the best.

Number One Doesn't Take any Crap

On the playground of business, Number One doesn't let anyone bully them around. *Go BIG* companies have no problem going up against the biggest kids on the block and making their presence known. They don't run scared at the first sign someone else might threaten them.

If you're going to be known as a Number One company you just can't take any crap from anyone. You need to be willing to claim your position at the top and hold it at all costs. If you don't, you open the door just enough to let your competition slip through, and that can become an enormous problem.

The problem with being "at the top" is that you are the #1 target for anyone who has any intention of succeeding in your industry. You become the team to beat, which is a full time position. Before you become the "Gooch" and scare little Arnold Jackson (c'mon, you have to remember that one – from Diffr'nt Strokes?) off the playground, though, you need to prove that you are willing to stand up to anyone and claim your position. Here's how the boys over at PayPal did it when their "Gooch" (eBay) pushed them around.

PayPal versus eBay

Today we think of the online payment service PayPal as a core component to the auction service eBay. Millions of customers use eBay to find goods and PayPal to pay for them. It's a beautiful union, so it may surprise you to hear that these companies were not always married. In fact, they used to be head-to-head competitors.

When PayPal was still a scrappy startup in the late 1990s, eBay noticed that many of its customers were using PayPal to pay for items purchased on eBay. As a result, eBay launched its own service – Billpoint – to provide the exact same service.

When they heard that their Number One customer was going to switch to an in-house platform most companies would have folded right there. But not PayPal.

Instead, PayPal actually fought eBay on their own site, in user forums, and throughout their marketing efforts to make sure PayPal was a viable payment alternative to Billpoint. They rallied the millions of PayPal users that they had collected on eBay to force eBay's hand and make sure PayPal could stay alive.

In fact PayPal not only stayed alive – they grew. They weren't afraid to stand their ground and fight against the very same company that was providing their customers. In the end they won. eBay purchased PayPal for over $1.5 billion and ended up replacing their own in-house solution with the very company they were fighting against.

www.paypal.com

Go BIG companies become Number One because they are willing to fight tooth and nail for their positions, no matter who challenges them. They don't fear the competition and they don't fear the biggest bully. They take them head on and are willing to fight to be the king of the hill.

You can get to a Number One position in ten minutes by some doing some fancy positioning, but actually defending that position takes a great deal of time, energy, and perseverance. If you're going to go all the way, you've got to be prepared for the fight ahead!

Recommendations:

- Let your presence be known. If someone is invading your space, go right after them head on. The more you let your competitors take advantage of you, the more they will do so. You need to let competitors know that if they intend on invading your space, they are in for a real fight

- Fear no one. Just because your competition is huge, it doesn't mean they are invincible. The most frightening thing to a bully is the person who is willing to fight back even harder. ("Now we know - and *knowing* is half the battle!")

Summary

In my travels I've seen lots of companies that really do want to think and act like Number One, but rarely do they actually market like Number One. That's generally because marketing like Number One isn't some creative idea you have in a meeting room, it's the day-to-day tactical aspect of actually making it happen.

It's also something that doesn't wear off. Nike has been in business for decades and yet they still spend all of their time reminding you why they area Number One brand. Creating a Number One brand is a commitment to establishing that brand not only in the short term, but over the long term as well.

Final Thoughts

Acting like Number One is the very essence of what makes *Go BIG!* companies so exciting – they strive to dominate their industries from day one.

As I spent some time digging into the backgrounds and histories of companies like PayPal and NetFlix what resonated with me the most was the fact that the founders of these companies didn't just *act* like Number One – they really believed they *were* Number One.

While I think you can manufacture positioning statements and market categories, I don't think you can manufacture the blind devotion to such a belief. Sometimes this blind devotion leads would be *Go BIG* companies right off the cliff, like Wile E. Coyote chasing the Road Runner.

But more often this notion of thinking and acting like Number One is the very spirit that makes these companies such dominant forces. The spirit that is often started with the founder of the company soon spreads like a virus throughout the rest of the organization and becomes the culture itself. I look at industry stalwarts like Microsoft and Apple and think about how the founder's enthusiasm and relentless drive to be Number One has propelled those companies to such great heights.

By all means I want you to think and act like Number One. But if I leave you with one parting thought for this section it would be this – it's all meaningless if you don't actually believe you are that company. Without the belief it's all smoke and mirrors.

Capital.

Create Capital

If you read popular business publications, you would think that raising lots of capital is synonymous with growing big companies. It would be hard to think otherwise, since most companies on their way to IPO riches seem to be surrounded by an entourage of venture capitalists and investment bankers.

But the real question is what did these companies do long before their star began rising so quickly? How did they get from the point where they had a big idea to the point where someone would even consider funding them?

This section is about everything that happens in the world of getting capitalized *before* you ever actually get capital. Incidentally this is where 99% of the startup world actually lives at any given time! I'd like to think this discussion will be helpful to a lot more startups than talking about what eBay did in the year before they went public.

Whether or not you raise capital for your startup company, you still have to deal with acquiring the resources you need to grow and launch your company. Finding these resources and knowing how to create the capital you need can make or break a startup.

What we'll cover in this section is how to think about the entire process of acquiring capital differently. I'm hoping that by the time you finish this section you'll begin thinking about every need you have for capital as an opportunity to create it out of thin air.

That may sound like some sort of magic trick but it really isn't. It's just a way of thinking about capital in a whole new light. Now before I start sounding like Yoda trying to explain the "ways of the Force" let me just jump right into what creating capital is all about.

Chapter 12

Get Resourceful

Instead of talking about how to raise as much money as possible to "get big instantly" we're going to go the opposite route – how to raise as little money (or none at all) in order to grow your company in its early stages.

Don't get me wrong, at some point in order to grow quickly you'll probably need more capital at hand than your business is currently throwing off. At that point it will make sense to go out and raise capital to *Go BIG* faster. But not just yet.

Startups tend to think they need tons of capital in order to become successful. Certainly this myth was perpetuated in the 1990s when venture capital investments were synonymous with successful startups. But the reality in a post-boom economy is that a startup can do far more with far less capital.

Even if I did say that capital was the answer to your startup needs, I'd really only be addressing a very small population of startups. Most startups get to market with little or no capital, but you never hear about those stories because there's no press release going out saying "XYZ company just raised ZERO capital!". Hopefully this chapter will be a little more relevant to all of those companies who never issued that press release.

The New Capital Climate

Since the bust of 2000 and beyond we've noticed a few key changes in the climate for raising capital:

- Investors are looking for companies that can demonstrate they are both profitable and resourceful.

- The cost to start a company is a fraction of what it used to be.

- Startups can do far more done with far fewer resources.

A combination of factors has played into this new climate for raising capital. Gone are the days of the bulky, cash-laden startup with tens of millions in venture capital and a hope that one day they might find profitability.

They have been replaced (read: forced into) a model that demands not only *rapid* growth but *responsible* growth. At the same time the costs involved in starting a company have become a fraction of what they used to be. The world is a lot cheaper. For this reason startups just don't need to raise money like they used to.

Don't get me wrong, they still need the same stuff – people, technology, and such – they just don't need to spend a whole lot of money to do it. I spent more time talking about the sweeping changes in the capital climate for entrepreneurs in the Introduction, so I won't bore you with a repeat visit.

Let's first dig a little deeper into the changes that have occurred in the last five years that have shaped the climate for raising capital. Then let's take a look at how this new climate has bred a different type of approach to raising capital – *creating* it.

Investors want hungry startups, not fat ones

If you begin your startup journey with $20 million in freshly invested capital at your disposal, you can tend to avoid worrying about things like making payroll on time, customers being a few months delinquent on their bills, and not hitting your revenue projections. And that's a huge problem – you *should* be worried about those things.

Investors aren't looking to bankroll companies so they can live high on the hog and hope that one day the business model turns profitable. Those days are long since over. Companies now must prove they can become profitable *before* they find an investment or die trying.

Investors are looking for companies that have demonstrated that they can create a product and find a few customers even with little or no money. Call it the Darwinian Law of Startup Evolution – the strong ideas and managers will survive while the weak ones will get thrown to the wolves.

By proving that your startup can make it past the early struggles of a startup's infancy you have also gained a great deal of credibility in the eyes of investors. Investors want to know that their money is going to be well spent on concerns that will lead to great profitability, not more perks for the executive suite.

The world is a lot cheaper

At the same time investors have become stingier about letting go of cost, the world itself has gotten a lot cheaper. When I started Blue Diesel in 1994, the cost of a basic PC was north of $2,000. Getting T-1 speed broadband access to our office was over $2,000 per month. A beefy Web server for our clients' sites was over $10,000. And the cost of a Web designer worth his salt was over $70,000 per year.

Contrast that to today's cost. I can now get a PC on eBay for less than $100, broadband access for about $40 per month, a Web server on a hosted platform for less than $200 per month and a Web designer for $10 per hour. And guess what – they all perform better than what I was paying for just a decade ago!

The Internet has done a nice job of delivering a whole host of services to our doorstep that lower the cost of starting a business considerably. You don't need one million dollars to start a company anymore. You need one thousand.

Even marketing costs have come down significantly. With the advent of online marketing there is truly a pay-as-you-go model for growing your budget. You can begin a campaign on Google for $15. Search engine and blog marketing is basically free. The power of word-of-mouth on the Internet gives you the opportunity to reach out to millions of potential customers at little or no cost.

Raising lots of capital to start and grow a company just isn't as necessary as it was ten years ago. The cost of resources has been reduced so much that a smart startup should be able to fend for itself well into its early maturity before capital becomes a requirement.

Startups can do far more with less

The very definition of going *BIG* no longer means *being big* physically. It means growing your market share without adding a sea of humans in cubicles along the way. Startups have more leverage in the marketplace now because of how much more efficiently they can market and scale their businesses.

Market leading startups are seeing a massive emphasis on speed to market, not size of infrastructure. Whether you're Craigslist dominating the market for online classifieds with fewer than 20 people or Google taking on Microsoft with a few thousand people, these companies are often a fraction of the size of their competitors, yet are consistently leading them in their respective markets.

The focus for startups is to do as much as possible with as few resources as necessary. Give partial credit to the evolution of the tools necessary to create and grow a startup. Whereas it would have taken a team of ten programmers and designers six months to create and launch an e-commerce website in 1995, the same work can be done today by a single person in a week.

This shifting emphasis on staying small is good news for the startup that can now focus less time and energy on placating investors' concerns and spend more time and energy placating customers' concerns.

The New Formula: Creating Capital

With all the forces of the startup economy shifting us toward smaller, leaner, and more resourceful companies, it's time to develop a new formula for the capitalization of startups – *creating* capital, not *raising* it.

Entrepreneurs often confuse the need for resources with a need for capital. While it's true that capital can help you purchase the resources you need, it's a means to an end. Creating capital means understanding what the end game is and trying to solve that problem, ideally without raising money to do it.

If you looked around the makeshift office of a startup, you would probably think that the company doesn't have much to leverage as far as capital goes. Not so. A startup has a great deal of latent capital just waiting to be extracted and used to solve the next problem or take advantage of the next big opportunity.

The trick is knowing where to look and how to leverage and extract it. More importantly, you need to know how to *think* about capital differently. So let's start there.

It's not all about the Benjamins

Let's first agree that money doesn't solve problems. OK, so you're probably thinking that money solves lots of problems. In fact, you wish you had some more of it right now to take care of some problems you have today!

While I'm sure the problems certainly exist, let's agree that money buys the *resources* that you need to solve the problems. What you really need is access to those *resources*, preferably without spending any money to get them.

For example, let's assume you need to acquire more customers (don't we all?). You may start by thinking, "I need some capital to hire some salespeople to get more customers."

You would be on the right track, but you would be missing the whole picture. What you *really* need are the salespeople who already have the connections to paying customers who are willing to buy your product. You're not buying people as much as you're buying *access to paying customers*.

Even still, you're probably now saying, "but I still need capital to hire those salespeople to get access to those paying customers!" Not exactly. What you need is an incentive, which doesn't necessarily translate to a salary.

That same incentive could be a commission plan that significantly rewards salespeople when and if they complete the sale. So what your problem really needs is a strong incentive compensation program, not a pile of money.

Get Creative

What we're really talking about here is identifying the resources necessary to address the problem, and then finding the most economical way to acquire those resources. There is no hard and fast rule about how it's done every time, although in this section I am certainly going to give you some ideas. The focus, though, is on looking at every opportunity as a way to *create* capital, not raise it.

This method of thinking doesn't end with just one problem. It's an entire mindset that should extend across everything that you do, and your approach to the overall growth of your company.

Smart entrepreneurs are resourceful entrepreneurs who can find creative ways to solve problems. Not only will being creative help you tackle more problems, it will also put you in a much better position to raise real capital if and when you need it. We'll talk about that later.

Money is expensive

Every time you forgo the opportunity to create your own capital and decide to take on outside capital there is a significant cost. There is the cost of your time to raise the capital, your loss of focus while you're raising capital (and not expanding your business), and of course the cost your equity stake if you trade equity for cash.

Let's go back to our salesperson problem. Had we decided to raise capital to find that salesperson we would have spent at least a few months talking to investors to get them interested in funding this initiative.

Not only would this have delayed the time to hire this person, it would have cost us time that we spent with investors when we could have been spending that time with customers.

And last, once we did raise the capital, we would likely face the dilution of our equity in exchange for it. Or perhaps we would have created more debt in the form of loans. Either way, we would be worse off financially.

Now think about our creative solution. No time spent with investors, we would have the person on board selling to customers immediately, and we would not have suffered any dilution or debt.

That's a very large difference in outcomes for solving a single problem. Add those across all the problems a startup is trying to solve in every aspect of the business and all of the sudden you've got a huge chunk of time, energy, opportunity, and capital out the window.

Create capital first, raise capital last

Now that we're focused on creating capital first, and raising it last, let's talk about the details of how we get from the point of being inventive to the point where we realize it's might be time to call some investors. I've broken this process down into four steps, from being broke and disciplined to going out and raising cash.

Stay Broke - being lean forces you to be disciplined. It's hard for anyone on the team to forget about being profitable and acquiring customers when no one is getting paid!

Create Capital - a startup has lots of latent capital. Learn how to create the capital to finance the things you need.

Find the Silver Bullet – before you can raise capital you need to know exactly where that capital is going to be applied and how it is going to make your company explode with growth.

Raise capital last - when you've exhausted every other opportunity, then raise capital. When you do, know how to act responsible about raising it and using it.

Chapter 13

Stay Broke

You may be looking at this chapter title and thinking, "Wil, I don't know why I'm reading this – I'm having **NO** problem staying broke!"

Staying broke may sound like a problem most startup companies face because of failure, but instead we're going to talk about this state of affairs as a strategy for success. You see, nothing reminds us how important it is to generate income like being flat broke! And that's the kind of focus we want in our company.

A dollar bill is a blindfold

Like I said before, having money in the bank keeps you from worrying about things like making payroll, having your customers pay their bills on time, and covering rent. And that's the problem. Those are things you *should* be worried about even if you *do* have money in the bank.

You should always be conscious of whether or not you are getting paid on time, whether the people on your payroll are carrying their weight, and whether you actually need the things you're buying for the business. That's healthy.

Most problems in business can be solved by throwing money at them, but that doesn't necessarily mean that's the solution. Throwing money at problems is for people who can afford not to think of more creative solutions. A startup doesn't fall into that category. With limited resources you need to conserve as much cash as possible and absolutely spend the time it takes to figure out those tough situations.

Being broke means being disciplined

It's hard to make poor investment decisions when you have no money to begin with. Having little or no cash forces you to find creative solutions to solving problems that larger companies would just throw money at.

Being a broke startup means having to learn the discipline of conserving cash, focusing your efforts on revenues, and getting it all done as quickly as possible – or else!

You may find people in the company that don't share your same fiscal responsibility. They tend to think of company money as Monopoly money that can be pissed through like water. But I can assure you that the first time you miss payroll due to poor financial planning they'll understand the value of being conservative really fast. Some people don't understand cash flow, but everyone understands *not eating*!

For this reason you need to make sure people understand that the same dollar you save by buying a slower computer or a cheaper desk is the same money that is there when it comes time to offer a Christmas bonus.

In fact I remember one time having a discussion with the founding members of a company and one of us was complaining about not getting a paycheck this week. That's when our accountant pointed to him and said, "you want to know where your paycheck is? You're sitting at it! It's the desk we bought for you last week!" Point well made.

Recommendations:

- Start broke and stay broke. Not having money to cover expenses forces you to focus on and address the real problems of the business, like getting customers and driving revenues.

- Use the "broken state" of your company to keep your entire team focused on generating revenue. Be quick to demonstrate that the extra hours they put in on the weekends directly translate to accelerating the rate at which they will get paid.

Raising Capital Costs Time

Every moment you spend kowtowing to another investor about your potential opportunity is a moment you weren't in front of a real customer trying to make a real dollar. Startups can spend months if not years trying to find an investor, only to let the market opportunity – the whole reason they were raising capital to begin with – slip right past them.

The more cost-effective climate of today's startup market means that more companies can self-capitalize and enter the market faster than ever before. That means by the time you've figured out who *might* invest in your business, a faster, savvier competitor has already bootstrapped their product into the market.

Instead of worrying about finding investors, worry about getting the company's products to market and proving the model. The time you spend actually getting the company to market will be much better rewarded than trying to sell a business plan to investors. In fact it's the investors who are the ones who want to you get your product to market and prove that it sells in the first place!

Recommendations:

- Skip the *capital* raising and get to *customer* raising. The time you spend raising capital could cost you the lead you need to get to market quickly.

- No matter how you slice it, it takes a great deal of time not only to raise capital but to manage investors once they are on board. Ask yourself – do you really need the additional overhead to be successful?

Summary

Don't look at being broke as a negative. Look at it as being "optimized for profitability." Being broke removes the luxury of being able to make decisions that don't affect the profitability and health of the company. And that's exactly why you want to stay broke for as long as possible. This position forces you to stay intensely focused on one thing – becoming profitable.

While we ultimately want to race to get to profitability and big riches, it's important to understand how being broke shapes the character and focus of a company for the better. Growing a great company isn't just about the executive corner office and the perks of ownership. It's about creating a living, breathing enterprise that can compete and sustain effectively over the long term.

A well-bred company, like a well-bred champion racehorse, is grown from day one with as much discipline and drive as possible. Being broke can create a tremendous amount of discipline to turn your little pony into a champion purebred stallion!

Chapter 14

Create Capital

Creating capital is about finding any possible way to cover the cost of a resource without actually spending a hard dollar to do it. The process by which startups create capital isn't some magical formula or "get funded quickly" scheme. It's an approach that companies adopt that basically says "wherever there is a need to fill, we will creatively find a way to fill it without using cash to do it."

Most people think that getting around the basic necessities of starting a business – hiring people, marketing your product, and acquiring customers – must absolutely require raising capital. I find this is rarely the case. The truth is that most startups can find the capital they need to grow their businesses right within their own businesses, they just need to know where to look

Human Capital

For any startup, raising money to hire people is always a problem. There's a lot to be done, and inevitably it takes people – who are very expensive – to do it. But how do you get the money to hire the people if you don't have the people to create the money in the first place? It sounds like a vicious cycle.

The key is to reverse the trend – to turn people into money.

Finding out how to bring staff members on board before you have a chance to pay them in real dollars will allow you to convert their time into money. In order to do this, you need to understand just how elastic the cost of people really is.

The Elastic Cost of People

The interesting thing about the cost of people is that while they are the most expensive resource you can buy, they are also the one resource that has the potential to cost nothing at all. A startup company has a unique currency – potential – that is used to convince people to trade their valuable time for little or no up-front compensation.

If the 1990s taught us anything, it's that sometimes the *potential* of what a company can be tomorrow is worth far more than a paycheck is today. Companies like Amazon, Yahoo! and Google have reminded us that trading a steady paycheck for a potential jackpot can be a great bet.

These companies and the people who worked for them recognized that taking a risk in the form of lower compensation in the formative years of the company would be worth it if the company took off. Even if you aren't planning on creating the next billion-dollar company, a modest plan that affords a healthy return for the time your people will put into your company is still a great payoff.

It's important to understand that the potential of your company is a real currency that can be used to buy many things, and people are one of them.

What you want to avoid is thinking that an hour of a person's time must immediately be compensated with a dollar out of your wallet.

Create paychecks of opportunity

Dale Carnegie's popular book *How to Win Friends and Influence People* provided one of the most important lessons for entrepreneurs looking to recruit talent who will work for nothing but potential – find out what motivates them. I said *them*, not *you*!

Everyone believes they are worth more than they are being paid. We want to believe that one day we will finally get properly rewarded for our hard work and become fabulously wealthy. Unfortunately very few of us have a distinct and obvious path to get there.

As a startup company you have the potential to fulfill that dream and many others. The currency of "potential" and the opportunity to change the world is a fantastic motivational force that you absolutely need to leverage in order to convince anyone that they should work for free.

Although a big payout is a great start, remember that people are motivated by lots of things, not just money. The right title, job responsibilities, or terms of employment such as flexible hours can be as much of an attraction as money. You must understand the needs of your people in order to create a startup opportunity that makes sense for them.

Paying people in the form of opportunity takes on well-known paths such as "stock options" and "equity stakes" that are synonymous with startup growth. Don't be afraid to use these tools in order to attract the resources you need to build your business.

I like to think of a stock option like a "paycheck of opportunity." Although you cannot pay real dollars now, the opportunity that the work everyone puts in will (hopefully) translate into a much bigger paycheck in the future.

Recommendations:

- Focus on connecting the value of your opportunity with the interests of the people you want to work with.

- Leverage your potential opportunity in exchange for people's time. People will work for a lot more than just a regular salary. It's important to know how to translate your opportunity into that paycheck.

Marketing Capital

Next to human capital, the question I get asked most often is how to create marketing capital in a business. Creating marketing capital may seem like an impossible task at first glance. How can you create capital for marketing if you haven't done any marketing to get revenue to begin with?

The answer lies in exploiting the aspects of your marketing strategy that don't necessarily require a big capital outlay to get started. The Internet alone has brought a billion people to your doorstep through an incredibly cost-effective mechanism. The tricks of the trade that *Go BIG* startups are using may employ some fancy new technologies, but they all rely on some basic human behaviors in order to be really effective.

Word-of-mouth

Word-of-mouth has become supercharged with the growth of the Internet. Word-of-mouth used to refer to just that – one person physically telling another about your product. It was effective, but ultimately slow.

Nowadays word-of-mouth has become one of the most powerful tools a marketer can have, leveraging the connectivity of the Internet. Companies like Friendster, MySpace, and LinkedIn have used the power of word-of-mouth to create social networks – friends inviting other friends to join their websites – and grab millions of customers within a matter of years with little or no marketing outlay.

The power of word-of-mouth is based upon the value of your message. The more powerful your message or value proposition to a customer, the more likely it is that customers will spread the word. Startups that are complaining that they can't get their product "marketed" but do not have a word-of-mouth strategy are missing a huge opportunity.

There is no secret sauce for creating word of mouth. It's simply about giving people a reason to brag about your product. If your software product makes collaboration among graphic designs as seamless as ever, then send a copy to some notable graphic designers for free to get them using about and talking about it.

Great products have a way of getting the attention of more and more people. Look at the buying decisions you've made throughout the day, from the restaurant you ate at for lunch to the website you visited this afternoon. What influenced your decision to buy? In many cases it goes beyond advertising and through word-of-mouth.

Recommendations:

- Create a word-of-mouth marketing strategy that gives your customers a reason to tell their friends about your product. A powerful word-of-mouth strategy will yield far better results than any traditional media campaign.

- Start with the key influencers who are most likely to tell other people about your product. People tend to get their purchasing behaviors from thought leaders who set the trends.

Leverage the Float

Some startups can actually grow their marketing budget simply based upon the use of their cash "float." Float is a term that refers to the time between when you incur an expense and the time in which you actually pay for it out of your cash flow.

You leverage float every time you make a purchase on your credit card – your credit card company pays for it now and you pay the credit card company back later.

Startups use the same concept to extend their credit to pay for media costs today, earn a sale, and then pay their creditors months later when the bills are formally due. At Swapalease.com we used this strategy to grow our marketing budget from $3,000 per month to $30,000 per month in our first year.

We simply paid for our marketing (mostly online marketing through Cost-Per-Click and similar services) through our credit cards and started generating traffic to our site immediately. That traffic was converted into revenue within 30 days, meaning we were making money faster than we were actually paying it out. We used that model grow our budget like crazy, basically "creating" capital along the way.

The strategy isn't particular to Swapalease.com or even online companies. For your company it's simply a matter of figuring out how long your sales cycles are –from the time you spend a dollar to acquire a customer to the time when you get paid by a customer – then figuring out how to stretch your payables to extend beyond your sales cycles.

Recommendations:

- Quantify the time between when you pay to reach out to a customer and the time when you actually get paid by that customer. That's your sales cycle and you always want to be making it as short as possible so you can turn cash over quickly.

- Focus on extending your credit terms for paying for your media or marketing expense so that they exceed the length of your sales cycle. This way you can earn money faster than you're paying it out.

- The key to growing your marketing budget is re-investing your earnings faster than you are paying for earnings.

Customer Capital

Customer capital is the value you create for your company and your idea by getting real customers to buy your product or service. When I talk about creating customer capital, people often respond by saying, "yeah, that just means revenue. Of course I should create that!" And to a large degree they would be correct. It is about creating customer revenue, but what's more important is how valuable that revenue is to your company.

The value of a dollar earned

A dollar earned from a paying customer is worth far more than a dollar raised from an investor. When raising capital you are really putting all that money to work so that in the end, the customer will pay for your product.

A paying customer alleviates all of that risk and capital and gets straight to the foundation for why you are running a business to begin with – to make money. Not only does this offer a more direct impact on the value of your business, it also keeps you from diluting your equity position in your company.

When you begin raising money in order to make money you're adding far more cost to the equation. Now you need to make up for all the capital that has been invested by creating even more revenue. You're actually making your job harder.

Customers on the Cheap

Go BIG companies know that getting a paying or active customer in the door is more important than anything else. For this reason they come up with creative ways to get their initial customers on board with little or no cost. Once a company has customers who are using and (hopefully) paying for the product, the company has far more value.

Before I go too far down this path let me point out that I'm not advocating giving away valuable service for free forever! That would violate all the stuff I spent so much time in the Vision chapter talking about. No, I'm saying that if it costs you $30 to acquire a new customer than perhaps giving away the first month of service for free (versus $20 retail) is more cost effective than paying the $30.

What we're trying to do is acquire customers as cheap as possible in order to create more value when they are all added together. That's what customer capital is all about, creating the aggregate value of having lots of repeat customers and having done lots of business.

Remember that just having lots of customers is one thing – have lots of *paying* customers is certainly another!

Netscape: A little free goes a long way

Netscape Communications found an effective way to use customer capital in their heyday. In a time when software companies were judged on the strength of their sales, Netscape did the unthinkable – they actually gave away their software for free.

While industry pundits laughed at their strategy Netscape ultimately had the last laugh. Netscape quickly developed a market share in the Web browser market of over 90%, launched one of the most successful IPO's in history, and sold to AOL for nearly $4 billion, all based upon the massive amounts of customer capital they raised.

While I'm not advocating giving your product away for free, it's important to understand how Netscape leveraged their customer capital in a most ingenious way. Consider how much it would have cost them to bring a paid version of their product to market and drive customer acquisition that way.

Now consider the cost to Netscape if another company had offered it for less (or for free) or if they had not achieved market dominance at all. In the end Netscape's customer capital was so valuable that even after losing the browser wars to Microsoft's Internet Explorer they were still able to sell the company to AOL for $4 billion. Most of us can only dream of one day making a mistake that nice.

www.netscape.com

It's not uncommon to hear about companies giving away a taste of their product in order to create the momentum they need to get bigger customers or more market share down the road. Remember that every customer you acquire without additional investment is worth far more than one acquired with additional investment.

Recommendations:

- Look for ways to drive customer acquisition at little or no cost. Remember that what you are making on those customers today may not be as important as having those customers so that you can get the next customer in the door to pay for your product.

- Having a big base of customers has intrinsic value. When valuing a company investors look at what it would otherwise cost to acquire that many customers on their own and attribute a company's customer volume to a real capital asset (even if no one is paying yet). Having lots of customers is worth something.

Chapter 15

Find the Silver Bullet

Once your company is up and running and you've created the capital you need to get to market, the focus now becomes validating the model and proving you know what it takes to scale quickly.

This is where *Go BIG* companies become *Go BIG* companies. They find out exactly which aspects of their model work (and allow them to scale quickly) and then move on to raising capital to help drive those growth factors as quickly as possible.

I'm not suggesting that raising capital is a must, but it certainly isn't appropriate until you've proven you've got a business model worth raising capital for. I see far too many entrepreneurs wasting far too much time trying to raise capital when what they should be doing is figuring out what about their business model is worth raising capital for.

Up until this point you've made some assumptions that customers will buy what you're selling and that the metrics for growth will hold up. Now it's time to prove you know what you're talking about! In this chapter we are going to figure out what aspects of our business model are going to be the "silver bullets" that will absolutely destroy our competition.

Validate your Business Model with Customers, Not Capital

A disciplined company looks to validate its business model with customers, not capital. Anyone can go out and raise someone else's money – that only validates an investor's willingness to part with their cash. The true validation of a business model comes when customers actually write a check for the product.

When a company is dead broke it has no choice but to validate the concept with customers, and that's good for everyone. This will force people to work on what is truly valuable to the future of the company – paying customers who like the product.

This is the time to focus your efforts on getting people to fork over cash for your product. There is an imperceptible gate you pass through when you get past the point where people are talking about buying your product and the point where they actually buy it. On the other side of that gate is your validation that the business model works.

What's nice about having paying customers (even if just a few) is that it allays the number one concern investors are going to have – "can these guys actually sell it to someone?"

Every business model can sound great on paper, but your ability to demonstrate that you can actually execute on the model will make you a far more favorable target for investors.

Recommendations:

- Put all of your time and energy into getting paying customers, no matter how big or small. A business is just an idea until someone buys the product.

- The most important assumption in any model is whether or not someone is willing to pay for your product. Just because you sign up lots of people or get lots of press doesn't mean anyone will pay for the product. Look at what happened to Napster.

Load your Silver Bullets

The silver bullets in your plan are similar to the growth factors. Remember, the growth factors of your business are the key drivers that, if tweaked properly, can give your company the boost it needs to grow faster and stronger.

Without knowing what the key drivers of the company are ahead of time, raising capital to expand the business becomes very difficult to do. Not only will investors balk at putting money into a plan that doesn't readily identify the growth factors, but even if you do get capital you will be throwing it down the drain if you don't know exactly how it's going to grow the business.

You may find that marketing at certain trade shows provides a healthy return on your investment, but you need more capital to attend more trade shows next year. Or you may find that your product could be far more cost competitive if you performed a larger manufacturing run that would cost a large chunk of change.

The closer you can tie your need for capital to immediate growth and scale in your business the better off you will be. If you don't really know how much it costs to acquire a customer or what your margins will be when your company grows to ten times its current size, you really don't have a silver bullet handy.

At the stage in your business where you're up and running and trying to prove the model, identifying and isolating your growth factors should be your most critical focus. Until you have proven that you understand what it takes to scale the business quickly, you are not only unprepared to scale the business, you shouldn't even think about raising any capital.

Recommendation:

- Isolate the growth factors of your business that will make or break your growth. Focus your time and effort on those factors and nothing else. If you can't seem to make an impact on your business by influencing the growth factors *before* you raise capital, it's not likely that capital is going to solve your problem!

Summary

This part of the equation doesn't require tons of explanation. It's as simple as this – if you don't know exactly how capital is going to take your company from Point A to Point B, you're not ready to raise any.

You may be thinking in more general terms, like, "I know that I need capital in order to grow," but that's too general. You need to know precisely where that capital is going to be applied – which marketing campaigns, which management positions, and which key orders. But you need to know a lot more than that.

Knowing where you are going to spend the money is easy. Knowing exactly how that money is going to translate into a big profit is what investors really care about. That's the part of the model that you are really trying to prove.

Chapter 16

Raise Capital Last

It may sound like this whole formula leads up to the inevitable end of raising outside capital, but it doesn't. In fact I'd like to amend this title to be "Raise Capital Last, *if ever at all*" but it doesn't look as good in the Table of Contents.

Even the smartest companies can only avoid outside capital for so long. The reality is that most hot markets are fiercely competitive, and time is the most critical barrier to growth. She who grows fastest wins.

For this reason most companies realize that the only way to grow faster than their current organic growth allows is to add more capital. That's a good reason to raise capital – when you know capital will create more profit or growth than you could otherwise achieve on your own.

So when the time comes that you've proven you've located the silver bullet in your business, you've validated the model with some real paying customers, and you've found yourself at a point where the only thing that can force you to grow faster is to add more capital, it's time to talk about raising money.

There are plenty of books that will tell you all about raising capital, negotiating term sheets, and managing your investors. This isn't one of them. Instead I'm going to talk about *when* to pull the trigger on your capital-raising activities. I believe that many startups find themselves looking for capital at the wrong time and that's what makes the process so long and difficult.

Let's talk about determining the most opportune time to take advantage of your capital-raising opportunities.

The Startup Law of Trajectory

Knowing when to raise capital is as much about knowing "when you're hot" as anything else. Startups have telltale signs in their growth that suggest the company is heating up. I'm not talking about well into your maturity after you've gone public or when the media has gotten a hold of your story and is promoting you like crazy.

I'm talking about long before you take on any investment or become huge. When you're just a baby but it looks like you might be the next Tiger Woods based upon some early indications of performance.

Your stock is hottest when it looks like your business is just about to take off. I call this the "Startup Law of Trajectory." The trajectory is the most probable path your business will take based upon rapid change happening now. More than any other stage of your business, the startup stage is the most likely to experience accelerated change.

As you see your customer base explode, revenues multiply quickly, and your popularity skyrocket, your growth trajectory looks as if it could shoot them to the moon, even though you may still be underground.

A startup's opportunity to raise investment capital peaks when a company is on the verge of showing a growth curve headed sharply upward – like a hockey stick. Investors jump at the idea of investing in a company that is about to skyrocket like this.

Because there is less upside potential in a company who has already experienced this potential growth, it's important for entrepreneurs to take advantage of their situation as soon as they see explosive growth on the horizon.

Look at those curves

Putting the Law of Trajectory to work begins with identifying recent trends in your business that can convince investors your business is gaining steam. We're talking about actual recent performance, not growth projections with no demonstrated history.

Anyone can project performance on a spreadsheet, but starting with actual performance creates a more compelling prediction for investors. It demonstrates that you have generated results and can quickly do so again.

The trajectory of your business may be evidenced by a variety of data. It could be the rate at which you are acquiring customers, an increase in profit margins as you grow, or simply revenue increases. What you're looking for are the metrics in your business that have performed well in the short term and are poised to spike in near future.

Let's say you just launched a new software product and put your beta version up for download on your website. If in the first week ten people downloaded the app, then 100 in the next week, then 1,000 in the next week and so on, you've spotted a growth curve that gets really interesting.

Perhaps only a few people have actually bought the registered version of the software, so sales aren't all that impressive, but the rate of adoption is incredible. That's the kind of growth curve we're talking about. Wherever your business is experiencing significant momentum in a fundamental metric is worth reporting.

That's what investors are looking for – some kind of trend that supports the notion that opportunity is just about to strike. And that's the kind of trend that you need to be spotting in your own business. A trend that suggests opportunity is about to strike and investors should get in now while the getting is good.

Recommendations:

- Determine what trends are fundamental to your business – rate of adoption, (declining) cost of sales, critical mass, etc., and track those. These will be the early warning signs that indicate your business is about to take off.

- As soon as you see a trend that looks like it could have a significant impact on your business if it continues in its trajectory, that's when you have something to sell. Until then, you're just another company trying to prove its model.

Build the Base to Increase Trajectory

Your recent performance is the most salient indicator of your future potential. It doesn't matter that a year ago you had a good quarter. That's history.

Investors are interested in recent performance and opportunity, not the past. Ask yourself, would you invest in the stock of a public company because they looked like a good investment a year ago? Probably not. Most likely, you would invest when a company has fresh success and demonstrates they can parlay that success into quick exponential growth.

From an investor's perspective, your stock is the most valuable when your recent performance plots an impressive trajectory. By demonstrating a track record for growth and a very bright future ahead of you, you gain leverage to find and negotiate the capital you need to take your company to the next level.

Let's go back to our software application. If it looks like the rate of adoption (the rate at which people downloading and using the software) is doubling every week over the course of six months, that's a fair amount of data that would suggest that people will continue on this path into the foreseeable future. The more data you have to support the base of the growth curve, the more credible the extrapolation becomes.

It's your job to find a point in your existing growth that supports your future hypothesis. There's no hard and fast rule that say it has to be a month, a quarter, or a year. Generally speaking the more data the better, but in high-growth companies a year of history tends to be a lot of data.

Recommendations:

- Now that you know what your growth factors are, look for performance trends that you can cite to support a future growth trajectory that will get investors excited.

- Remember that it's your trajectory they are buying, not so much the actual recent performance. It's not about the fact that 1,000 people downloaded your application, it's that based upon the rate of adoption you can predict 1,000,000 people will download it by this time next year.

Sell Fast 'cause it Never Lasts

Being on an accelerated-growth trajectory is like being the biggest new star in Hollywood. You've got all the potential and all the attention. But like most stars, yours may not burn brightly forever.

All you need is a single quarter of poor performance to turn your growth curve upside down. Then, for as much as the curve helped you to become a potential giant, it could sink you by making your track record and credibility look spotty at best.

The art is in the timing. You need to recognize positive growth trends early enough to begin promoting them and converting them into well-negotiated investments. The longer you wait, the greater your chances that something may go wrong and throw your growth path off track.

While you're hot, begin making your pitch to investors to allow them to see that you have a real business that has real, demonstrated growth. Focus on the fact that unlike other opportunities that promise the potential of doing something positive, your company has already begun building a foundation of success to launch forward.

The window for taking advantage of the Startup Law of Trajectory is fleeting, so getting your investors lined up and locked in quickly is what the game is all about. The fact is that no company can stay hot forever, not even eBay or Amazon. What these companies have done, and what you need to replicate, is taking full advantage of your future trajectory when the opportunity presents itself.

Remember that your trajectory is one of the most valuable assets available to you throughout the growth of your startup, so don't be afraid to leverage it to grow. Whether you're two guys in a room or about to take your company public, it's your future that has value. So go sell it.

Recommendations:

- You're always working against the clock when raising capital in a high-growth startup. When your window of opportunity presents itself, jump all over it and take advantage of the upswing. The startups that burn brightest burn fastest.

- Any quarter that paints a bad picture of your trajectory can sink you. No matter how rosy things seem to be going today, don't assume they'll stay that way forever.

Final Thoughts

The goal of this section was to get you to start thinking about capital differently. Not as an end but as a *means* to an end. Hopefully you'll be so resourceful with your capital needs that you'll never actually have to raise capital at all – that would be nice! Nothing is sweeter than owning the whole thing and not having to give up ownership to get what you want.

In the event that you do need to go out and raise some capital to grow bigger and faster I hope you can appreciate the little bit of insight I've tried to provide about the capital game. If you've noticed a recurring theme it's that raising capital is all about creating leverage early in your development so that you can give investors something to salivate over.

Starting a company isn't about hoping to one day placate investors (that's called "going public"). Starting a company is about keeping your focus on building great products, servicing customers, and hopefully making a nice, healthy profit in the process.

Management.

Stay Small

After we've put so much emphasis on what it means to build a *BIG* company, it may surprise you that we're going to wrap this book up by discussing how to stay *small*.

In this section we are not talking about how to restrain your vision or your growth – far from it. We're talking about how to focus on keeping the size of your infrastructure as small as possible while growing the revenues as fast as possible.

As new market opportunities pop up faster, it's becoming harder for big companies with enormous, bloated bureaucracies to rally quickly and take advantage of these opportunities. Instead, the opportunities are being exploited by smaller companies that can react much faster.

It's not surprising, then, that some of the biggest market opportunities – the Web browser, the search engine, and even the market for online music distribution were uncovered by very small companies, not large ones. These companies (Netscape, Yahoo!, and Napster, to name a few) were started by small organizations (college kids, actually) who knew that being small and fast was far more important than being large and "established."

Go BIG companies, therefore, are intensely focused on two things – staying small and making a big impact. They understand the value of speed and know that they don't need a lot of people or infrastructure to make a big impact in the marketplace.

We're not talking about how to stay small, but rather how to stay efficient. One of a startup company's greatest assets is its inherent ability to move quickly and efficiently. It's what makes startup companies so powerful early on. This section is all about how to stay lean and mean even as you *Go BIG!*

Chapter 17

Small is the New BIG

In this chapter I'm going to explain that in order to seize new market opportunities a company needs to emphasize being quick and nimble over being big and bulky. The paradigm of having huge companies dominate their respective markets has changed considerably. These days, small is the new *BIG*.

Back in the day, market opportunities were afforded almost exclusively to big industry behemoths that could afford to take advantage of them. You had to research products, build factories and spend millions on marketing through traditional media channels to bring these products to market. It took a great deal of time and a great deal of money, which big companies had lots of and startups did not.

But a lot has changed in the last decade or so. The Internet alone has given startups the power to bring products to market in record time at a fraction of the cost. The barriers to entry that once kept the industry behemoths at the top of the food chain have been largely destroyed making these companies incredibly vulnerable to attack.

Think of Big Companies like the Death Star

My best analogy would be to think of big companies like the Death Star in the movie *Star Wars*. The Death Star was big and powerful, with the ability to destroy an entire planet in one fatal blow. I mean seriously, look how easily it destroyed Princess Leia's home planet of Alderaan. It seemed like nothing could stand in its way.

But then along comes Luke Skywalker, in his tiny little X-wing fighter, descending upon the Death Star to destroy it. You would think that if the Death Star could blow up an entire planet, destroying little Luke and his X-wing would be easy.

In fact it's not so easy. You see, the Death Star was designed like most big organizations to be able to crush big competitors who also move slowly. When someone like Luke attacks, leveraging his speed and agility to run circles around the Death Star, the big hulking ship can't possibly mobilize quickly enough to defend itself. It gets destroyed before it even has the opportunity to react.

Large companies face this same dilemma. While on the outside they seem like the can destroy anyone, when you realize what it takes for a large organization to respond to an attack (or a new market opportunity) you will find that being little Luke has far more advantages.

The Three Deadly Sins of GiantCorp

Big companies have more weaknesses than ever before, particularly in markets that are evolving quickly. Look at what happened to the music industry just a few years after the first copy of Napster hit the Internet and downloading an MP3 song for free became a lot easier than buying one.

As a startup yourself, it's important to learn the weaknesses of these companies so that you can exploit them. Even more importantly, you need to know how to avoid creating those same weaknesses in your own company as you rise to power.

To illustrate the weaknesses of big companies, I'd like to pick on a fictional company called "GiantCorp." GiantCorp represents every big company with its bloated management and glacial pace of market responsiveness.

Sin #1: Middle Managers are like Molasses

The reason big companies can't respond quickly to new opportunities is due, to a large degree, to their inflated bureaucracies. It's a simple issue – the more people they hire, the more managers they need, and the longer the chain of communication becomes.

At the same time each of those managers feels they need to have a say in every decision that gets made. What used to be a small, smart, decisive company becomes a big, bloated committee of decisions makers (or "non-decision makers" as is more likely the case).

Big, bloated committees are not useful when trying to innovate in a marketplace that moves at lightning speed.

Let me show you an example of the difference between how "two guys in a room" can execute a new idea versus the bumbling machine that is GiantCorp.

Two Guys in a Room vs. GiantCorp

Let's say you and I come up with a fantastic new business idea. We meet for a beer, convince each other it's brilliant, and wake up the next morning with a killer concept and a killer hangover. Then we get to work.

Time to initiation = about 24 hours.

Contrast that with what happens in a big corporation – in this case we'll call it GiantCorp. You and I have a great new idea, but this time we are lowly peons in the big corporate machine. No matter what we come up with in our brainstorming session at the local bar, we can't go to work on it the next day.

Instead we have to get a hold of our respective managers and schedule a meeting to talk about the idea. They of course, in true *Dilbert* fashion, take it to their respective managers to "run it up the flagpole." And so on and so on.

At some point (months from now) the concept gets filtered up to a "decision maker" who is so far removed from the original concept that his view of its "brilliance" is simply lost. Whether he says "yes" or "no" to the idea is meaningless because by the time the committees are setup to make the call and the idea is approved the concept was already brought to market by the two guys in a room who actually got it done.

Time to initiation = about 6 months (probably longer).

As you can see, big companies are not built to respond to good ideas quickly.   Smaller players have the ability to think just as quickly as big companies, but more importantly they can act quickly.   Without any management to pass along their ideas, they can simply get it done.   This is why the technology industry is so loaded with innovation – it really only takes a couple engineers to turn an idea into a product.

Sin #2: "The Opportunity is too Small

The other problem these big companies have is the simple fact that they are big in the first place. Most big ideas start off as really small opportunities, and that's where the problem starts.

When big companies have to generate billions in revenues to meet each quarter's goals they don't have the luxury of spending time on hundred thousand dollar revenue opportunities. The problem there is that most new, innovative companies start out as just that – hundred thousand dollar opportunities.

A hundred grand happens to be a lot of money to two guys in a room but worthless to a division that has to generate $100 million in revenue. That's why a company like Yahoo! (or for that matter Google) can pop up almost out of nowhere.   A small search engine is a great project for a small company who can see value in even $100,000 in revenues. That might be worth working 24/7 to create.

But $100,000 in income barely pays the catering bill for a big company, so it gets overlooked by "mature opportunities" that can have proven they can generate far more revenue today.

Thus, two guys in a room create Hotmail and sell it to Microsoft (who should have thought of it) for $400 million a couple years later. Or a few guys in a room create MySpace.com and sell it to News Corporation for over $500 million a few years later.

Startup companies often overlook this fact. They assume that if they see how big the market opportunity is that their bigger competitors must see it as well. Even if the larger company does see the opportunity, being able to get the support necessary within the organization to respond to the opportunity is an amazing challenge.

Sin #3: Too Many Moving Parts

Let's say that at 3:00 in the morning the GiantCorp CEO wakes up and has an epiphany for a great new product that could make a gazillion dollars for his company. With this in mind I suppose we could say that he could get around Sin #1 (since he is the decision maker) and even Sin #2 (since he would determine the opportunity is big enough).

But even with all of his power, the poor CEO of GiantCorp still can't get over one simple fact – the organization has too many moving parts. The moving parts of GiantCorp involve HR managers, IT managers, Marketing managers, and so forth. The organization relies on lots of people and processes in order to function effectively. And that's exactly the problem.

In a big organization all of these parts have to move in unison in order to get something done. Let's go back to our Death Star example for a second. When Grand Moff Tarkin (the executive manager of the Death Star) wants to move the Death Star to blow up a planet, it's no big deal. They can take their time and get everyone in line to move the Death Star.

But if Grand Moff Tarkin needs to move quickly to respond to a single, fast moving threat, he has to get all of his subordinates moving in the same direction at the same time. He may get it done, but it won't be fast. He's doomed.

By contrast, a startup has none of that baggage. Two guys in a room can get to work on their idea and have a prototype to show customers by the time the Director of Marketing is done coordinating with the CIO of GiantCorp.

Big companies like GiantCorp are ultimately built to sustain and grow existing products, not to innovate new ones quickly. Because of this, as the organization grows and adds more moving parts, it actually makes itself less likely to mobilize quickly on new market opportunities.

Summary

I wanted to dedicate an entire chapter to illustrating how companies like GiantCorp are so incredibly vulnerable to smaller, faster companies. In the chapters that follow we're going to get into some strategies about how to stay small and nimble so that you don't end up becoming that big, bloated behemoth.

Beyond that I wanted to also demonstrate that you don't need to be intimidated by big companies. For all of their many assets, their relative size and lumbering pace can make them much less formidable adversaries than you may think.

Go BIG companies not only recognize the weaknesses of these big companies, they prey on them. They look for every opportunity to exploit these companies. In fact, some *Go BIG* companies are designed from the ground up not only to exploit the weaknesses of their competitors but in fact to become an acquisition candidate by the very same companies.

For all their weaknesses, the one major asset that big companies have is their checkbook. Microsoft is notorious for losing market opportunity after market opportunity to smaller companies, but they are just as well known for buying the very companies that outmaneuvered them.

However you decide to position your company in the long term, the one asset you cannot afford to lose is your speed and responsiveness. These days the best way to *Go BIG* is to stay small!

Chapter 18

Leverage your Smallness

Startups and small companies have one incredibly powerful asset – their ability to make decisions quickly and mobilize their forces all at once. This sense of market dexterity can allow seemingly tiny companies to become forces to be reckoned with if they leverage their smallness in just the right way.

As the changes in business markets continue to happen faster, the quick and nimble are becoming more valuable and better rewarded than the slow and powerful. If positioned correctly, a small company can find ways to outfox companies many times their size.

I like to think of smaller companies as if they are using "Business Judo." The principles behind Judo allow you to use leverage to knock your opponent off balance and use their weight against them.

Let's also bring our scrappy little contender, VideoBlog out from the Growth section as the new student – the Karate Kid to my Mr. Miyagi. I want to demonstrate how VideoBlog can knock down much larger competitors by simply leveraging its smallness – acting faster and using speed to its advantage.

Of course we are going to go toe-to-toe with the feared GiantCorp, our fictitious "big" company that is used to smashing little companies like ours into smithereens.

Get inside their decision cycle

In the military there is an expression known as "getting inside the enemy's decision cycle." It means that you are reacting so quickly to the changing environment that you are making moves before your competitor can make a decision about your last move.

A small company can leverage its speed to react to market conditions before a bigger competitor has even responded to the last change. By the time these companies have responded to your last market offer you are already rolling out the next feature or product.

Let's use this concept to take some shots at GiantCorp with our new VideoBlog service. Now we know that GiantCorp is interested in getting into our space, but they haven't actually launched the product yet. We're in the same boat. We want to get into the market but our product is also still in development. Let's see what we can do to use our size to our advantage.

Spread the word first

Being in the ad agency business, I was always amused at the channels and processes that existed when it came to getting an "official word" of any sort out to the public. A document as simple as a press release, something that takes some PR person an hour to author, can literally take months to issue.

When GiantCorp wants to make it known that they are going to get into the video blogging space, they have to traverse lots of channels long before they can get the word out. In that time the media (and the buying public) is waiting around for someone to announce they are going to be in this space.

By the time GiantCorp has drafted the release, sent it through a chain of managers, had legal review it, contacted partners about potential conflicts, re-drafted the release to reflect potential conflicts, notified all departments of the announcement, and sent the release to their agency to distribute, we've long since announced our position in the space.

Being first-to-market is critical because it forces all other entrants to the market to be considered as "follow on" products, which suggests they are taking our lead. That's a nice position to be in considering we're a fraction of the size of GiantCorp. The point is that we can move faster to make simple marketing decisions like a product announcement long before our big competitors can even finish getting approvals.

Recommendations:

- Look for opportunities to get the word out before anyone else, especially larger competitors. You have the advantage of being able to communicate quickly and efficiently, so use it.

- Make it clear in your communications that you are the leader or the first. A great deal of attention is conferred upon the companies who are first to market, especially in developing markets.

Feature Faster

In a world dominated by "upgrades" and "new features," releasing new features faster means creating the perception of a superior product. Once again it's time to use our size to our advantage to roll out new features and upgrades faster than GiantCorp.

By the time GiantCorp has gotten consensus from their "strategic managers" about the direction of their video blogging tool, has allocated capital expenses and resources toward the project team for the tool, and has finished testing their new ideas with focus groups, once again we've already released our new features.

By comparison, VideoBlog (our scrappy team of two guys in a room) turned their chairs around, settled on the five new features that the company should have (while eating lunch) and then spun around again to start developing those features. Weeks later the new features were released. This was at about the time the CTO of GiantCorp got around to re-arranging the project schedules of some of his developers so that he could brief them on the new feature requests.

Making quick decisions isn't just about sending press releases. It's also about being able to quickly come to consensus on key product changes and get them rolled out quickly. Most larger companies have lots of moving parts. The moving parts are required to make the larger engine hum, but they don't create the most efficient mechanism to get smaller projects done efficiently.

In this case I'm suggesting you roll out features quickly, but the same strategy can be used to modify any aspect of your business faster than your larger competitor. The key is knowing where they are deficient and striking at that point.

Recommendations:

- Look for opportunities to make small, incremental improvements that your customers will notice faster than larger companies. To your customers you will appear more adept and innovative.

- Even small product changes can lure customers away from a competitor's product. While GiantCorp is busy rolling out a big "version 2.0" their customers are still looking for a solution to their problem today. Never underestimate immediate gratification.

Concentrate All Firepower

Going back to our *Star Wars* analogy, it's important to point out that Luke Skywalker never tried to go head-to-head with the Death Star. Instead he concentrated his firepower on a known weakness that could not easily be defended against. Small companies need to operate like Luke Skywalker in this case.

Let's assume that our VideoBlog service was trying to go head-to-head with GiantCorp. In this case let's say GiantCorp is a company like Yahoo! that has an enormous amount of visitor traffic and lots of existing customers and services.

If we tried to build a service with the breadth of Yahoo! we would get crushed. There's no way we could possibly offer all of the features and services they do. But if we focus on what we do really well – video blogging – we would stand a much better chance at beating them.

Small companies need to learn to concentrate their firepower on particular targets versus trying to play at the same level of their much larger competitors. While Yahoo! might try to integrate their video blogging service into a hundred other services they provide, we will focus on building the best possible video blogging service and nothing else.

Concentrating your firepower means rallying all of your resources – people, strategy, and marketing dollars – around one particular goal. Most large companies will have a much harder time trying to compete as effectively on one highly-targeted product or service since they need to pay attention to many products or services simultaneously.

It's also a lot easier to do one thing really well versus trying to do lots of things really well. Concentrating your firepower also means getting the benefit of laser sharp focus toward a particular goal. Sometimes the focus you put on one particular problem or goal alone will allow you to be inherently more innovative.

Recommendations:

- Don't spread yourself too thin! Instead, pile up all of your time and energy on one particular product or service and be incredible at that one thing first. Your best bet is to stack your resources behind the battles you are most likely to win.

- If possible, look for potential weaknesses in your competitor's lineup. If you find out there are only a handful of people supporting a product that could be a key opportunity for you, go after that. You want to hit the hardest where the resistance is the weakest.

Chapter 19

Stay Small

Believe it or not, it's hard to keep the size of a company as small as possible while trying to grow as fast as possible. There seem to be unlimited opportunities and the only way to take advantage of them all is to add more people and more infrastructure.

The fact is the bigger you get physically the more unwieldy and lethargic the organization becomes. *Go BIG* companies aren't trying to add as much headcount as possible – quite the opposite. They are looking for ways to keep headcount low so that they can operate faster and more efficiently.

I've had the good fortune to lead great companies from two people to over 500 people and I can tell you first hand that the bigger they get, the harder they are to operate efficiently.

Fortunately there are some very deliberate approaches you can take toward keeping the company lean and mean even as it grows. A word of warning, though – these are approaches you will need to implement over the long haul – they aren't quick fixes! A company that intends on staying at its "fighting weight" needs to constantly keep in shape.

Avoid Bureaucracy like the Plague

Startups have the ability to instantly communicate across the organization – literally! Swapalease.com has less than 20 people on staff and they all sit in one room without any walls. When there needs to be a change in strategic direction you can literally address everyone at the same time immediately. It's a pretty efficient way to communicate.

A large company cannot possibly do this. Large companies like GiantCorp tend to gravitate toward "layers of management" with hierarchical reporting structures that are slow and filtered.

The last thing you need as a *Go BIG* company is layers of management and longer reporting chains. I've seen this happen, too. I've seen startups with ten people who already have a management reporting chain from the CEO to a VP to a "line worker." For some reason these companies feel like they should *reduce* their speed of communication as quickly as possible!

Startup companies should avoid this type of bureaucracy like the plague. Any structure that slows down communication within the organization is hurting it. Startups need to maintain their quick communications and open discussion policy as a key asset.

Here are some ways to help reduce the bureaucracy in your own organization:

1. **Report "in," not "up."** You need as many open lines of communication as possible. There is no reason why an intern shouldn't be able to walk in the CEO's office and share his mind. Every time someone has to report "through" someone else to share their ideas you slow down communication and risk filtering valuable input.

2.   **Get a room**. Yes, get a room – just one. By that I mean *do not* get individual offices that keep people from talking to each other regularly. At the Go BIG Network, for example, anyone in our office can see what I'm doing from their desk (and vice versa). You'd be surprised how many more ideas are shared when someone doesn't need to compose an email just to say something. (It also keeps people from surfing eBay all day.)

3.   **Take away titles**. Titles give people a sense of entitlement (what a surprise, right?). People seem to love having big titles to confer their importance, but I will say in a startup they do more harm than good. Who cares if you are the VP of Marketing if there isn't anyone in your department? If people think they need a title to confer respect or authority then they really don't have any to begin with. Instead of conferring titles upon people, simply give them responsibilities. It's a lot harder to hide behind responsibilities than it is a title.

Keeping the organization light and well-communicated is not hard to do. It just takes an understanding and appreciation of good communications. The very asset that allowed you to outmaneuver your larger competitors by reacting quickly and making split-second decisions could be the one that destroys you when you give it up to the next "new guy."

Recommendations:

- Do everything humanly possible to keep the bureaucracy out of your organization. It may find its own way in, but you don't need to accelerate the process!

- Take advantage of the ability to speak to everyone at once. If you can't get everyone in one big room on a daily basis then try pulling them into one room at least on a weekly basis. The more opportunities you can create to share ideas, the better.

Remove the Human Element

I know this might sound like a directive from Montgomery Burns of *the Simpsons*, but it's not quite as dire as it sounds! In order to keep the company light and nimble, you need to avoid adding people-intensive processes.

Most companies solve problems by throwing people at them. For example, when more phone calls start coming into the call center a CEO might immediately think, "we need to hire more phone support personnel!" It's times like these when I want you to ask yourself, "can we solve this problem without hiring more people?"

It's not about being stingy with your payroll. It's about being efficient with the use of your resources. Take a look at a company like Craigslist.org that services millions of customers per month with its online classified ads and forums. Did you know that they handle all of this volume with just 18 people? I asked the founder, Craig Newmark how they did it. Here's what Craig told me:

"We're trying really hard to keep our company growth very slow, since dysfunction grows with size, using some techniques including:

- More "self-serve" functionality, which people prefer anyway.

- Continuous improvement of the way we do things. For example, customer service people figure out how to work smarter, than ask tech to improve their toolset."

As you can see, it's not about removing people necessarily. It's about putting them in positions to be more effective so you don't have to *add* more people. Here are a few places where "removing the human element" can really help out:

1. **Teach customers to fish**. Look at what Craig said about customer service. Instead of staffing more people to answer customer calls and requests, his team looks for opportunities to let customers help themselves. It's like the old adage about teaching a man to fish. Give your customers the tools they need to service themselves so they don't need to be more reliant upon you.

2. **Hire fewer robots**. Every company hires robots. They are the people who do exactly what they are told to do – no more, no less. The problem with hiring robots is that they don't think about what they could do to avoid having to do the same task over and over. They see getting the task done over and over as a "good job." What you want to find are people who will look for creative ways to let technology or some other mechanism do the task for them.

3. **Automate everything.** These days you can automate a hell of a lot of processes that used to take people to do. Whether it's setting up an automated kiosk for customers to purchase from you or building an online knowledge base for customers to answer their own questions – automation is everything. At the Go BIG Network we spend 99% of our time building tools to keep us from ever having to repeat that process again. Think of automation as progress, and manual labor as failure.

Ideally you would run your organization without ever having to hire any additional staff at all, but that's not likely to happen. Instead, with a focus on removing the human element in every aspect of your business, you can feel confident that when you do go to hire someone, it's because they can create less work for everyone, not just inflate your payroll.

Recommendations:

- Look for every possibility opportunity to take manual processes *out* of the process. Anything that can be done with some other service or technology *should* be done by some other service or technology.

- Be proud of how small you can keep your staff. Big companies with big payrolls are fat whales waiting to get speared. *Go BIG* companies are proud of their margins, not their payrolls!

Lighten your Load

If you were to pare down most companies to just the people who actually produce and deliver the product you would be surprised at how little those companies really are. Over time companies add people to perform all kinds of tasks from payroll to customer service to IT implementation.

The problem with staffing up more full-time employees to handle all of these roles is that they become horribly distracting to the core business which is delivering quality products to customers. Not only do they add more people to monitor they also require a great deal of time and expense to staff, train, and retain.

A *Go BIG* company doesn't really need all of this extra baggage. These days the answer to fulfilling requirements that are outside the core business of the company is simple – outsource it!

Outsourcing isn't simply about saving costs, although if you're lucky you can save a few nickels while you're doing it. Outsourcing is about saving *time* and *focus*. Even large companies with lots of cash have only a limited amount of time and focus. Outsourcing allows you to push those activities that do not drive the business forward off to the periphery so you can maintain a razor sharp focus on your product and your customer.

Once again we want to develop a mindset of "if it's not core to the business, we'll find someone else to do it." Every problem that you can solve by pushing it out to your periphery brings you one step closer to gaining total focus on your core product.

Here are some places that startups can begin to remove non-critical processes from their plate:

1. **Clerical Tasks.** This should be an easy and obvious one. Most tasks like payroll, billing, travel planning, and the like can and should be moved to an outside firm. They are probably not only better at it – they'll be more cost-effective in the long term.

2. **Find Partners.** Even the delivery of your product can be streamlined by finding partners who can service non-essential aspects of your product offering more efficiently. For example, at our ad agency Blue Diesel we offered everything from Web design to email marketing to Web hosting. But we didn't actually do all of that work in-house. We found partners who were better-equipped to deliver these services and paid us a cut of the new business generated. It worked out better for everyone and allowed us to grow our core product which was strategic Web development.

3. **Temporary Everybody.** Not every new project or customer engagement requires you to hire everyone onto your payroll full-time. When possible, try to augment your full-time staff with consultants, contractors, and part-time personnel. The great thing about temporary staff is that you are not beholden to them if things "go bad" (and they do) but if things go well you've already had time to test them out in case you want to offer them a full-time position.

The list of places to outsource jobs and lighten your load is endless. But it starts with the goal of trying to maintain as much focus as possible by keeping non-essential tasks and personnel out of your day-to-day view.

Look around your office today (if you have one) and ask yourself, "are we spending even one minute on tasks that aren't directly tied to delivering a quality product to our customer?" If the answer is yes, you know where to start making some changes.

Recommendations:

- Make a list with two columns – "stuff you do that directly relates to delivering a quality product to your customer" and "stuff that doesn't."

- Run down the list of "stuff that doesn't" and think of alternatives to performing these tasks yourself. Then you can begin reducing the size of the organization and staying small.

Chapter 20

Stay Focused

The definition of a startup means you have very few resources to employ and little time to get them to do something valuable. The clock is always ticking, and the money (if you even have any) is running out by the day. With so little to leverage, you need to make sure that the focus of your company's product offer is as razor sharp as possible.

At the same time most startups have very few resources to mobilize. You really can't afford to run off in ten different directions at once. Staying focused is as much about strategically positioning your company as it is about making the most efficient use of the limited resources at your disposal.

A startup in its formative stages is like a newborn baby – it has the potential to become anything. And that's the problem. You're lucky enough in this lifetime to be the best at one thing. Maybe it's golf and your become Tiger Woods. Or maybe it's software and you become Bill Gates. But you're not going to become a champion golfer and a software tycoon at the same time (although many of us are trying).

That point is that a startup company needs to stay focused on being the best at one particular thing – whatever that "thing" happens to be. In this chapter we're going to look at the strategies and related benefits of staying focused in the short term to make the best use of your size.

Don't "be *all* you can be" – be as "*little* as you can be"

Most startup companies fail because they try to be too many things to too many people. They think of every possible option they could load into their product offer. While this may give them the feeling of being one of the "big boys," the grim reality is they are not. In fact by trying to be too many things from the start, these companies often end up delivering *less* value!

PayPal: Really Good at One Thing

Instead of trying to be all things to all people, try being one thing to all people. Think of PayPal, the highly successful startup that allows users to email money over the Internet to each other. PayPal could have chosen a million options for their offer.

They could have become an online credit card company, an auction site, a loan provider, and so on. But what made the company successful was their focus on only one offer – emailing money from one person to another.

PayPal understood that their ability to do one thing really well would help set them apart. For a while they even competed with auction giant eBay, the very same company who ended up purchasing them for $1.5 billion in 2002. eBay launched the very same service (emailing money) on their auction site. But eBay was busy being an auction company, not a payment services company. By staying focused on doing online payments better than anyone, PayPal was able to build a huge following of loyal customers – most of who, ironically, came from eBay.

www.paypal.com

You don't win medals (or customers for that matter) for rolling out as many features and being in as many markets as humanly possible. Almost every major company that has gone *BIG* has done so by focusing on one particular product or opportunity and completely kicking butt at that.

Microsoft made its money and its fortune as an operating system long before branching off into word processors and X-Boxes. Nike made its money selling great sneakers (they still rule) before branding MP3 players. The point is great companies start by building a highly-focused cornerstone business and then expand from there.

Recommendations:

- Sit back and take a look at everything you're doing. Can you point to one thing that you are intensely focused on? Or are you trying to get twenty things out the door? I think you know the answer to this one.

- Is everyone at the company intensely focused on that one thing? Or is everyone running around doing their *own* thing? Your resources are always limited, so it might be time to get everybody working on the same project!

Bite off less than you can chew

Delivering your product to market is an amazing feat. Even still, a common problem among small companies is their inability to predict what it will take to actually support a product once it has gone to market. It's easy to conceive complex products with lots of features. But actually bringing that product to market and supporting its use with customers is a whole different story.

Instead of trying to roll out everything and the kitchen sink in your approach to market, just roll out the sink. If you find that you can support your product just fine after it's been successfully selling in the first year, then go ahead and add to it. It's a lot easier to add features along the way than it is to support features you don't have the resources for.

Let's take a look at what would happen to our little VideoBlog if we got aggressive too quickly.

VideoBlog: Too Big for its Britches

As brilliant entrepreneurs we sat at the kitchen table and conceived an unbelievable business plan for VideoBlog. We decided we were going to be the next NBC or ABC with enough content to support an entire channel on the television dial. We put the time and energy into launching a service that could take over the world!

Then we launched it and people actually used it. Soon the phones were ringing off the hook with customer complaints, vendor solicitations, and more customer complaints. We were in constant triage mode fixing all the bugs that were created in our haste to get the product to market.

Instead of growing the product and the company, we got buried with service calls trying to support our massive creation. While we were caught keeping this thing running, our faster, more focused competitors were quickly refining a more streamlined product.

That's a short version that doesn't get into the details but hopefully doesn't belabor the point. A small, efficient startup needs to maintain its greatest asset – "being efficient." When you bite off more than you can chew by launching too much product too quickly, you run the risk of getting buried with your own creation.

Instead, try taking smaller bites of projects that you know you can complete and manage. Like a big dinner, you can always take another bite. But once you've swallowed too much, you'll choke.

Recommendations:

- Pare down your objectives and projects into just a few small items that you can knock out quickly and move on to the next ones. You can always add more.

- It's nearly impossible to anticipate how hard it is going to be to actually support what you've sold, so just assume that it's going to involve a lot of time that you won't have later. By releasing "less" product you will give yourself some time to understand what it will take to support the product – which is always a lot!

You have Ten Seconds to get it Right

Your customer has a life, even if you do not. They are constantly bombarded with marketing messages from the latest movie releases to the newest type of shampoo. They don't have the time or energy to stop their entire day to focus on your product. So if you are lucky enough to have ten seconds of their attention, you had better make good use of it.

The exercise of focusing your value proposition into ten seconds (or less) is a great way to distill your feature set to those items that will get people's attention right away.

If it's not going to add value to the ten-second pitch, it's not critical to your product's success. If you can't get your customer's attention with the one key benefit to your product, the rest of your features won't matter anyway.

Debbie Does Everything (the realtor)

OK, first get your mind out of the gutter! We needed a catchy title for a realty service not an adult movie! Now picture Debbie's residential real estate business. Debbie is incredible at selling houses in her local market, but she thinks it would be great to market herself as the realtor that does everything.

Debbie not only wants to sell your house, she wants to help find contractors, relocation services, even a babysitter in case you need to go house-hunting while she's selling your existing home. And that's really cool, there's only one problem – no one will ever know that.

You see, when people are going through yellow pages looking for someone to sell their house, they have one item on their mind – selling their house! They are going to look for the realtor who looks like they will provide the best possible opportunity to sell their house. The fact that Debbie does everything is great, but all her customers really care about is selling their house.

If Debbie were to distill the value proposition for what she does into ten seconds, she couldn't (and wouldn't) possibly want to cover every possible thing that she does, even if Debbie really does everything. She'd want her customer to know in ten seconds that she sells houses better than anyone, so she should focus on that!

Like Debbie, your startup company is in the same boat. You can't assume your customers are going to care about every last thing you do. They only care about the things that you do that have particular importance to solving their one core problem.

Recommendations:

- Without thinking through it first, tell me right now in ten seconds exactly why I should choose your company to do business with.

- Now, write that pitch down and compare that to all of the features and services you offer your customers. Are there a whole bunch of them that didn't make it into the pitch? If so, those should be the first activities that get put on the back burner until you're absolutely confident that I'll buy from the product you pitched in ten seconds!

Summary

Your product launch is just the beginning of trying to keep your focus. Once you have taken your product to market and enjoyed some early success, it may become even harder to stay focused.

Now you have customers calling you and recommending (or demanding) features to be added and services to be provided. All of these distractions make it harder to keep your team focused on a single goal.

Fortunately the process of keeping your resources focused post-launch is entirely the same. You need to pick your battles and allocate your resources toward the few initiatives that will do the one thing right that is truly driving your company. Serving the needs and whims of every customer sounds great, but it can also be a terrible detour when trying to maintain the forward progress of your company.

If at any point during your journey you're unsure whether or not you're spending your time and resources effectively, just ask yourself one question: "Is this driving the core benefit of our product?" If the answer is "yes," you're headed in the right direction.

The Obligatory Epilogue

I never really understood the epilogue of a book. I've always figured that if an author needed additional room to make a point, she would just add another chapter.

I do a fair amount of public speaking and advising to entrepreneurs and those that want to get into the startup game. Often I am asked for some words of encouragement that would prompt would-be entrepreneurs (and those struggling through the rigors of the startup game) to *Go BIG*. These are my three most popular responses.

Reason #1: There's no money in a paycheck

I've always told people (usually when trying to recruit them from their current jobs) that if you know how much money you're going to make next year, then you need to find another job. That's because the jobs that are truly rewarding (financially) have virtually unlimited upside.

It's actually very difficult to get rich when you have a fixed income like a paycheck. Starting a company and going BIG is the only way to make P Diddy-type wealth. At some point the company needs to be working for you, not the other way around.

Reason #2: If you're not jumping out of bed, go back to bed

99% of the time I have a hard time staying asleep. It's not that I have insomnia or live next to a highway, it's that I am so excited about what I'm doing that my mind is constantly racing. During that time I don't even need an alarm clock to wake me up. I jump out of bed in the morning and can't wait to get to work.

That's how I know I'm doing what I should be doing for a living.

The other 1% of the time I wake up in the morning and wish the alarm hadn't gone off. I lie in bed, stare at the ceiling, and second guess all of the choices I've made in my life. That's how I know it's time to do something else for a living.

Reason #3: If you're not gonna go BIG, you may as well go HOME!

This point obviously inspired the book, so I thought it was fitting that it would be the last point that I would make. I don't think this reason applies to everyone and that's just fine. This is what works for me. Your own mileage may vary.

I've got 8 – 20 hours per day to spend working. I can choose to spend that time doing something that I think is marginally interesting or something that I think is wildly exciting. I can try to make my next startup a global powerhouse or keep it alive just enough to pay my bills.

The choice is mine. In my case I'm *not* interested in building a 2nd place company – I want to be Number One. Even if I don't make it, that's the goal. I believe that if I have one shot in this life to do anything, I'm going to give it everything I possibly have.

I believe that if you're not gonna *Go BIG*, you may as well go HOME. Buy hey, that's just me

Shout Outs

There are many people who helped contribute toward making this book a reality, both directly and indirectly. For this reason I'd like to give a special shout out to:

Joel Peach for editing, proofing and generally helping take this book from 900 pages of nonsense to a few hundred pages of slightly more sense.

And then of course there is Sara Sommer (for keeping me fed and sane), Ryan Mapes, Brian Campbell, Tyler Ransburgh, Eric Corl, MarKel Snyder, Craig Stein, and the rest of the Go BIG posse for basically putting up with me.

To all of my fellow entrepreneurs holdin' it down in the 614 – Pawan Murthy, Adam Torres, Andy Graf, Mike Breslin, Ross Youngs, Charles Penzone, Rich Langdale, Dennis Glassburn, Doug & Cookie McIntyre, Jim Moran, Nancy Petro, Chris Rockwell, Jeff Scheiman, Ray Shealy, Keith Singleton, Dwight Smith, John Wallace, Tony Wells, James Paat, Mike Mozenter, Janis Mitchell, Derek Harp, David Decapua, David Babner, Stuart Crane, Don Anthony, Charles Fry, Andy Dickson, Brad Howard, Jim McGuire, etc. etc.

To the rest of the world (because believe me, Columbus, Ohio really isn't the center of the Universe) – Dan and Carey Tedesco (and lil' Ev!), Chris and Rebecca Anzidei, Jeff Roberto, Chris and Danielle Bingham (and his hot mom), Ron Lewis, Jazz Sahota, Flavor Dave Ranallo, et al.

To all my partners in crime – thank you for believing in me – Sam Keller (Kelltech), Blane Walter (inChord), Damon Caiazza (LeasePower), Mike

Koulermos, Tim and Julie Harris, Kip Thomson (Powerhouse), Ken and Amy Rinaldo (Atomica), Alec Shankman (Status), Ron and Richard Joseph (Swapalease), and so on.

To the original Blue Diesel crew – Damon Caizza, Joel Peach, Joel Jimenez, Mike Klebacha and Jason Brua.- remember when turning 30 meant retiring?

To the people who helped and inspired me to actually get this book written: John Huston who introduced me to Jim Canterucci who introduced me to Toni Robino who collectively explained to me what it meant to get a book written.

To Dom Cappa and Don DePerro for believing in my work and my column.

And to my family and friends for being cool with watching me take a year and a half away from seeing them. I'd love to say it'll be the last time that happens, but you all know me too well!